MOSAICS IN ROMAN BRITAIN

MOSAICS
IN ROMAN BRITAIN
ANNE RAINEY

A GAZETTEER

DAVID & CHARLES
NEWTON ABBOT

0 7153 5791 3

Set in 10/11 IBM Press Roman
and printed in Great Britain
by the Pitman Press Bath, Somerset
for David & Charles (Holdings) Limited
South Devon House Newton Abbot Devon

TABLE OF CONTENTS

LIST OF ILLUSTRATIONS

PLATES

Geometric with dolphins, Wynford Eagle, Dorset *(Dorset County Museum, Dorchester)*   160

DRAWINGS
Over 60 drawings of motifs are printed in the Glossary.

FOREWORD

This gazetteer of Romano-British mosaics has been prepared for interested amateurs who have no classical background or previous knowledge of ancient mosaics; hence the detailed glossary and the general account in the introduction of the history of mosaic pavements. It has, however, been suggested to me that the book may also prove of value as a handbook for serious students. If this should be the case, I would ask them to overlook the elementary character of some of the information.

I have concentrated primarily on the visual aspect of the mosaics, by describing the designs in some detail and indicating where they may be seen, whether in situ, in museums or in illustrations. Where mosaics have been lost and no pictures of them are available, useful descriptions contemporary with the discoveries have been quoted. Some 750 mosaic pavements have so far been discovered in Britain and an Ordnance Survey National Grid reference is given in each case to indicate the approximate position of the site.

Pending the publication of a corpus of mosaics found in Britain, by Dr D J Smith of Newcastle-upon-Tyne, I hope this book, together with its Selected Bibliography, may help to promote a greater knowledge and understanding of the subject, and impress upon the reader how much of interest may be seen in town and site museums throughout Britain.

A.R.

INTRODUCTION

The art of laying mosaics was, so far as we know at present, developed by the Greeks in about BC 400, when small black and white water-worn pebbles were used to depict mythological and other pictorial scenes. This technique was later superseded by the use of small cut pieces of marble, stone, pottery and glass, known as tesserae, which gave the artists far greater scope for creating such complicated figured pictures as the well known Battle of Issus, found in Pompeii.

However competent the mosaicist may have been, the medium of mosaics seems to be insufficiently plastic to produce the soft shadings of colour needed for landscapes and figures. Whereas in frescoes and paintings the colours can be subtly blended, in mosaics, no matter how carefully the coloured tesserae are used, they must be laid one beside the other. It is precisely these clear-cut lines that are particularly suited to complex geometric designs, which gain their strong visual effect from the juxtaposition of contrasting colours and can therefore be admired for their intrinsic beauty as well as for the obvious skill of the craftsman.

Greek artists were commissioned to lay mosaics far beyond the boundaries of Greek-speaking lands and their work was particularly popular among the peoples of the Western Roman world, under whose influence the mosaic became less a medium for creative artistic expression and more a display of the craftsman's technical ability to copy designs.

Throughout the many centuries during which Graeco-Roman culture endured, the same basic motifs appear in mosaics, wall paintings, pottery, sculpture and metal work, with no great alteration or development of style. It is therefore difficult to believe that patterns were either handed down from master to pupil by teaching and example alone, or that each successive generation of mosaicists had access to original masterpieces for study and reproduction. Pattern books, compiled from these original designs and from copies of famous Greek works of art, and circulated through the mosaic workshops, are far more likely to have been the means of perpetuating these classical themes and motifs. A striking piece of evidence for this theory is the close similarity between the Bellerophon and Chimaera scene on the pebble floor laid in Olynthus in northern Greece in the late 5th century BC, and that which appears on the 4th century AD mosaic at Hinton St Mary, Dorset, in Britain.

The fact that none of these pattern books have yet been found is not, to

11

my mind, a reason for doubting their onetime existence, since they were probably made of such perishable materials as papyrus, parchment or even very thin pieces of wood. The books would not necessarily always have contained whole compositions ready for copying, but often just the outlines of a range of geometric designs and sketches of clothed and naked figures, busts, animals, flowers and trees, to be arranged and completed according to the ability and imagination of the mosaicist, who sometimes showed a marked lack of skill and understanding of the significance of the pattern or of the classical characters.

The first mosaics in Britain must have been laid by craftsmen, brought from Rome or elsewhere in the Mediterranean area, who may have trained local people to assist them. Then, as the demand for this type of work increased, workshops were probably set up in such towns as London, Verulamium and Colchester, which enjoyed prosperity in the early days of the province, and later wherever economic development led to the building and reconstruction of houses and villas on a large scale.

Dr D J Smith[1] has so far established the probable existence of four fourth-century schools of mosaic in Britain, which, he suggests, were situated in Corinium-Cirencester (Glos), Petuaria-Brough (E. Yorks), Durobrivae-Water Newton (Chesterton, Hunts), and Durnovaria-Dorchester (Dorset). His conclusions, which are of great importance, are based primarily on the evident similarity of style and content of the mosaics found in each area. He also suggests that workmen from the Corinian workshop may have been responsible for the Corinian-style mosaics found in other parts of the country and even as far away as Trier in Germany.

Although the craftsmen employed in any one of these workshops would have been trained by the master mosaicist, the standardisation of design in each area is so marked that it is likely to have been due as much to the use of workshop pattern books as to the personal influence of any one craftsman. If this were so, the mosaics executed in a style peculiar to one atelier, but found lying outside its area, would be more likely in many cases to have stemmed from the sale or exchange of patterns between the workshops than from a travelling mosaicist.

The more complicated figured medallions and panels in Romano-British mosaics may have been prefabricated in the local workshops, brought to the site in small portions and then reassembled, the whole composition having been drawn in situ, and the background finally filled in around them. Signs of this method of laying the pavement are thought to have been detected in the discoloration of the mortar at Hinton St Mary. Small *emblemata,* worked in minute tesserae, were made in Hellenistic workshops and taken considerable distances on trays of tile or marble to be incorporated in an all-over geometric surround, but only two sites in Britain are known where the central design is executed in tesserae markedly smaller than those forming the remainder of the floor. These are Rockbourne in Hampshire and Harpham in Yorkshire; but in neither place have trays been discovered, nor would the pattern have been sufficiently elaborate to merit prefabrication of an *emblema*.

Apart from beaten earth, flags and *opus signinum*, the most inexpensive form of flooring must have been coarse tessellation in one colour. This is found not only in the poorer houses, but also in the lesser rooms of villas and town houses where there were also patterned mosaics in the bath suites and living rooms. Practically all patterned mosaics have a border of larger tesserae, usually in one colour, from which the design could be viewed, so that presumably a floor with a wide plain border was less expensive than one with either a narrow surround in coarse tesserae or one executed entirely in fine tesserae.

Most of the raw material for tesserae came from various parts of Britain and included limestone (grey or brown), lower greensand (shades of green), sandstone (soft yellows), Purbeck marble (dark blues, reds and greens), Kimmeridge shale (black or dark grey), hard chalk (white) and pottery and tile, sometimes burnt (shades of red, purple and yellow). Coloured glass was rarely used in Britain and then only for a few tesserae which could add colour to such details as the tail of a peacock or the wreath of Bacchus; but a selection of loose glass tesserae, some sheathed in gold foil, was found at Capel St Mary in Suffolk. The material had first to be cut into portions and large cubes; an operation which may have taken place at a stonemason's, for pieces of sawn chalk were recently discovered on an industrial site near Corfe Castle in Dorset, well placed for dealing with raw material quarried in the Purbecks. Although manageable sticks of sawn chalk were found here and at Silchester in Hampshire, knapping was probably always the process used for hard stone. The task of sawing, knapping and sorting into suitable sizes and colours probably took place either at the stonemason's or in the mosaicist's workshop before the tesserae were brought to the building sites, although it appears that some of this work may well have been done on the site itself, as at King's Weston in Somerset. The careful selection of colours and of pieces to fit particular figures must have been carried out by the mosaicist himself, whether in the workshop or on the site. The tesserae were then set in a mortar bed spread over deep foundations of graduated materials on a rubble base, or on a thin layer of mortar on a natural base, the determining factor for this bedding usually being the stability of the subsoil.

Most of the mosaic pavements in Britain would have been laid by craftsmen operating from workshops and probably using pattern books compiled from a selection of designs, some of which may have been imported and others drawn by a local workshop artist. The unique Virgilian mosaic at Low Ham in Somerset appears, however, to have had an exceptional origin; inspiration for these scenes probably coming from an illustrated manuscript. Since neither the villa owner nor the mosaicist was likely to have possessed such a rare and expensive volume, it could be that a travelling artist, perhaps from North Africa, made sketches from an illustrated codex containing the Aeneid for use on this one floor. The fact that the same scenes have not so far appeared in mosaics elsewhere in the Roman Empire, tends to preclude the possibility of their having been derived from the usual imported or local pattern books; but Professor Toynbee has suggested to me that since very few illustrated Roman manuscripts have survived from the many which must have existed, it is possible that there was a Virgilian pattern book used by book illustrators and mosaicists alike. If this should be the case, other mosaics with scenes from the Aeneid, similar to those at Low Ham, may yet be discovered. The scene depicting the birth of Bacchus at East Coker, also in Somerset, and the interesting mosaics at Brading on the Isle of Wight, may also have been the work of a foreign mosaicist, since they do not have much in common with other mosaics in Britain.

Before the early years of the twentieth century, even the best excavators had little idea of the value of stratified coins and pottery for the dating of associated structures, and indeed nothing was known of the dating of pottery. This lack of knowledge was probably responsible for the excavations which were little more than treasure hunts, with the unearthing of a mosaic, a piece of sculpture or a coin hoard as their main objective. Where a date was assigned to a building it was usually as a result of the chance discovery of a coin or of a piece of inspired guesswork. Sites with mosaics which were excavated in this way should now be re-excavated using modern techniques, so that we may be able to form a more comprehensive picture of the chronology of Romano-British pavements.

It nevertheless seems likely that most of the mosaics in Britain were laid in two main eras, the first from circa 150 to circa 200 AD, a period to which belong pavements from several villas in south-east England, together with those in such towns as Silchester, Verulamium and Colchester. Mosaics of the 1st century AD, such as those at Fishbourne, Eccles and Angmering, where coloured tesserae were found in a late first-century context, are so far very rare.

As far as we know at present, the early and middle third century appears to have produced only a few mosaics, whether in towns or villas, although modern dating techniques may one day prove that far more were laid at this time than is now thought to be the case.

The later third and early fourth centuries saw considerable development in the construction and enlargement of villas and houses in some towns throughout the country. This inevitably led to an increase in the demand for mosaic floors and therefore to the establishment of new workshops. During this second period of activity figured mosaics appear to have become increasingly popular, particularly in the south-west and the north-east of England, where flourishing agriculture brought wealth to the country landowners and to the merchants in towns, which were basically market centres for agricultural produce.

It is important to bear in mind that no discovery made so far has proved beyond doubt whether the pattern book or the craftsman was primarily responsible for the uniformity of design found in the mosaics attributed to each of the workshops thought to have existed in Britain. If, however, we assume that pattern books were imported from the Continent and circulated among the workshops in Britain, we must be very cautious in dating Romano-British mosaics by stylistic comparison with Continental mosaics. A Continental parallel would usually give only the earliest possible date for its counterpart in Britain; similarity of design between British pavements need mean no more than the possibility that the same pattern book had been employed over quite a considerable period of time. Thus the firm archaeological dating of one pavement would not necessarily be a guide to the dating of another containing the same motifs.

Buildings in Britain are thought to have been mostly of one storey, half-timbered with stone foundations, varying greatly in their decoration. A number of houses had only plain tessellated floors and some had only one or two mosaics, whereas others, such as that at Woodchester, had at least twenty. In many cases the floors were laid over hypocaust basements in winter living-rooms and bath suites. This has resulted in the loss of many mosaics, which had collapsed into the hypocaust or been smashed by robbers taking brick or stone from the pillars supporting the floors.

Besides producing a number of very striking geometric designs, mosaicists in Britain drew quite widely on Graeco-Roman mythology for their subjects. Marine compositions with Neptune, fishes and dolphins were a particularly popular theme. Outstanding examples of these are the frieze of fishes in the ambulatory of the octagonal plunge-bath at Lufton, that surrounding Venus at Hemsworth and the 'scatter' of marine creatures from Dyer Street in Cirencester. At Fifehead Neville, in Dorset, where two rings with the Christian monogram were found, the fishes and dolphins surrounding a large urn or cantharus may have had a Christian significance. The cantharus, symbolic in pagan art of the mystic communion between Bacchus and those initiated into his cult, was readily adopted by Christians for the chalice, emblem of the Eucharist.

The Christian implication of many apparently purely mythological scenes has been the subject of full and authoritative discussion by Professor J M C Toynbee[2]. Such religious interpretations can be readily appreciated at Hinton St Mary, where Christ is portrayed in one central medallion, and in the other

Bellerophon spearing the Chimæra is, as in the later case of St George slaying the dragon, symbolic of the victory of truth over error. It is doubtful, however, whether all the scenes at Hinton St Mary and at Frampton, where there is also a Chi-Rho in the mosaic, were chosen with a specifically Christian purpose in mind, even if they were capable of a Christian interpretation. The newly converted Christian may have considered it prudent to propitiate several of the old gods by incorporating them in the mosaics, or his choice may have been dictated by purely aesthetic considerations, or even by the limitations of the available pattern book. There is also no firm evidence that the numerous mosaics with Orpheus surrounded by birds and beasts, particularly popular with the Corinian workshop, can, in Britain, be taken to represent Christ the Good Shepherd, although this is certainly true of several representations of Orpheus in the Christian Catacombs in Rome and on Romano-Christian sarcophagi.

Mosaics in Britain may not be as sophisticated or colourful as many of their counterparts in other countries, particularly those round the shores of the Mediterranean, but taken as a whole they provide important evidence of the extent to which Graeco-Roman culture and art had penetrated this out-lying province of the Roman World.

1   Smith, D J (1965) Smith, D J (Ant J 1969) Smith, D J 1969
2   Toynbee (PDNHAS 1963) Toynbee (JRS 1964) Toynbee (1968)

GAZETTEER

See Abbreviations pp 196-200

ABBOTS ANN, Hants
SU 3141   4th cent f   1854 (?)

Fragments stored in British Museum
Traces of a large villa were found and it was reported in *The Builder* of 1855
that 'Two rooms have been lately discovered, about 16 feet square, with a
circular ornamental tesselated centre-piece, 6 feet in diameter, in the middle
of each, being in form hearts within hearts, circles and points composed of
three different colours . . . the villa to which these rooms belonged, appeared
to occupy within walls, seven or more acres of ground . . . the pavements
have been removed to London . . . ' The fragments which have been preserved
are two medallions with stylised flowers and the corner of a rare chain pattern
border, the latter found also at Great Tew in Oxfordshire.
Illustration Hinks (1933) fig 130–1

ALDBOROUGH *(Isurium Brigantum)*, Yorks
SE 4066

A small *civitas* capital of some 55 acres was first enclosed by earth fortifications and later by a wall. The modern village of Aldborough, now occupying
the site, is considerably smaller than its predecessor *Isurium,* which must have
had many rich houses, judging by the number of mosaic pavements found
during the 18th and 19th centuries. Although good drawings of these mosaics
were made and published by Francis Drake in 1736 and by H Eckroyd Smith
in 1852, there is very little written record of the discoveries, so that only a
few can be sited with accuracy.
1. Three pavements, probably all from the same town house, were found
behind the Aldborough Arms.
a. f 1832   On view in situ   (Site Museum)
   A series of borders surround a small central square in which a lion lies
   peacefully beneath the spreading branches of a tree. H E Smith's
   drawing shows more of the lion than can be seen today.
   Illustrations Charlesworth (1970) pl 8 & Smith, H E (1852) pl XVI
b. f 1848   On view in situ   (Site Museum)
   An attractive square pavement has a central eight-pointed star or flower
   framed by a series of borders, including an unusual arrangement of
   alternate plain and Greek key swastikas.
   Illustrations Charlesworth (1970) pl 9 & Smith, H E (1852) pl XVII
c. f 1846   Covered over in situ
   A large apsed pavement is divided into three sections; an antechamber
   with a guilloche 'mat' leads to the main part of the room where only a
   corner, with a swastika border and a bust, survives. Unfortunately very
   little of the apse mosaic remains, but fragments of panels with robed

19

figures, one holding an open scroll, with the word *Helicon* in the background indicates that these were perhaps the nine Muses of Mount Helicon.
Illustration Smith, H E (1852) pl XVIII
2. 4th cent (?)   f early 19th cent   In Leeds City Museum
A panel from a larger pavement found near the east gate has, under a spreading tree, a primitive and childlike rendering of Romulus and Remus with their foster mother, the wolf. The twins, who appear to be dancing a jig, are disproportionately small, and the wolf seems to have cat's ears and a horse's body!
Illustration Toynbee (1963) pl 220
3. A pavement found under the vicarage was said to have been very fine.
4. f circa 1732
At Borough Hill, in the centre of the village, a number of geometric mosaic pavements were found and drawn by Drake.
Illustrations Drake, F Eboracum (1736) figs 1-4 & Smith, H E (1852) pls XII and XIX
5. f 1770
To the south of the main east-west street a long range of rooms was discovered. The corridor of assorted geometric patterns, drawn by Eckroyd Smith, may have come from this building.
Illustration Smith, H E (1852) pl XIV
6. Another corridor has the unusual swastika pattern with bars, also found as a border at Micklegate Bar in York, a guilloche bordered rectangle and a guilloche swastika.
Illustration Smith, H E (1852) pl XII
7. Panels of chequers and grid pattern interspersed with lozenges.
Illustrations Smith H E (1852) pl XIII & YAJ XII (1893) 420
8. H E Smith shows a large diamond outlined in guilloche, enclosing two stylised peltae and two hearts, in addition to two geometric designs already drawn by Drake in figs 2 & 3 above.
Illustration Smith, H E (1852) pl XIX
Many other pavements have been found and destroyed without record, but in view of the fact that *Isurium* is now so sparsely inhabited many more may await discovery.

APETHORPE, Northants
TL 0294   4th cent (?)   f 1859

Fragment in Central Museum, Northampton
A large circle within a square has round the outer border a series of small semi-circles, and the inner border has a motif resembling a necklace of Aladdin's lamps; within the central medallion are scrolled 'S' shapes in pairs and a plain square sparsely decorated with simple geometric forms.

In each spandrel are two rather clumsy sprays composed of lotus buds, cornucopiae (?) and leaves springing from a minute stylised urn.
Illustration VCH Northamptonshire I (1902) fig 20

BANWELL, Somerset
ST 3959   4th cent (?)   f 1967

A large hypocaust room in the bath house of a villa has a relatively small guilloche bordered rectangular panel between two half walls leading to the main part of the room; the contents of both were destroyed. Small fragments indicate that the room may have been divided by guilloche into a grid of twelve panels, one of which framed a stylised flower.
Reference JRS LVIII (1968) 199   No published illustration

BARTON FARM (Cirencester), Glos
SP 0102   4th cent   f 1825

In Corinium Museum, Cirencester
A villa situated just outside the walls of *Corinium* had a rectangular pavement composed of two panels of perspective box pattern flanking a large square holding a circle. In the central medallion is an attractive figure of Orpheus with a dog (?). The inner circle has a frieze of brightly coloured birds and is separated by a wreath of leaves from the outer circle, where life-like beasts prowl among bushy trees. In the spandrels are stylised leaf sprays and the whole pavement is bordered by swastikas enclosing panels of guilloche.
Illustration Smith, D J (1969) pl 3.12

BARTON-IN-FABIS, Notts
SK 5231   f 1830 (?)

The one mosaic found so far on this site, and only partially excavated, is rectangular with borders of red and blue. 'To these succeeded delicate double lines of white tiles, inclosing a magnificent scroll border, six inches broad, of interlacing red, white and blue tiles, succeeded by another double delicate white line. The centre part . . . is occupied with a great variety of geometrical figures, such as squares inserted diagonally within squares, others of the chequered pattern, others trapezial, and all centred in a large ellipse, the whole had a most brilliant effect.' The drawing of all that remained of the mosaic in 1881 indicates that this may have been of perspective box pattern framing medallions (?).
References Arch J XLIII (1886) 30 & Briscoe, J P Old Nottinghamshire (series 2) (1878) 143

21

BASILDON, Berks
SU 6079   f 1839

a. A guilloche-bordered square holds an octagon enclosing two large interlaced guilloche squares, which in turn frame a stylised flower in a
medallion bordered by cog-wheel triangles. Swastikas and winged duplex
knots occupy lozenges round the interlaced squares and each outer corner
holds a lotus flower.
Illustration Smith, C R (1848) pl XXIV
b. Concentric parallelograms in two shades of red and blue.
Reference Arch XXVIII (1840) 447

BATH *(Aquae Sulis)*, **Somerset**
ST 7564

The small Roman city of Bath, which covered 23 acres, owes its existence to
the thermal baths developed round hot springs in the first century AD.
Adjacent to these baths was a temple dedicated to the local goddess Sulis-
Minerva.
1. Bluecoat School   f 1859   In Roman Baths Museum, Bath
A fragment with sea-beasts and a dolphin was probably part of a scatter of
sea-beasts, and is so far the only figured mosaic to have been found in the
city.
Illustration Cunliffe (1969) pl LXXXIa
2. East Baths   Two heated baths, each in an apse, had mosaic floors.
a. f circa 1756   Lost
A fragment of swastika pattern bordered by triangles is said to have been
found in the western apse, but the pattern appears to have been ill suited
to a semi-circle.
Illustration VCH Somerset I (1906) fig 30
b. f 1923   On view in situ (Roman Baths Museum)
A fragment with a semi-circular border of triangles.
Illustration Cunliffe (1969) pl LXXXIIIb
3. Mineral Water Hospital
a. f 1738   Lost
An all-over pattern of interlaced circles.
Illustration Cunliffe (1969) pl LXXXIVa
b. f 1859   In situ
A fragment of corridor with a line of swastika pattern.
Illustration Cunliffe (1969) pl LXXXIb
c. (Bridewell Lane)   f 1884   In Mineral Water Hospital
Extensions to the hospital revealed a fragment of a more sophisticated
mosaic composed of a grid of octagons enclosing stylised flowers.
Illustration Cunliffe (1969) pl LXXXIIa

22

4. Royal United Hospital   f circa 1865

A central square panel, holding a stylised flower, has six narrow borders with patterns including castellation, tiny chequers and shaded awning pattern.

Illustrations Cunliffe (1969) pls LXXX & LXXXIIb

5. Weymouth House School   f 1897

A guilloche-bordered medallion, contents destroyed, lies in a square with lotus flowers in the spandrels and a border of swastikas enclosing squares.

Illustration Cunliffe (1969) pl LXXXIIIa

BATHFORD, Somerset

ST 7866   f 1665   Lost

A villa found on land belonging to a Mr Skreene had a mosaic described by John Aubrey. 'In the middle of the floor was a blue bird, not well proportioned, and in each of the four angles a sort of Knott *(sic)* . . . Mr S told me there is another floor adjoining yet untouched.'

Reference BFC V i (1885) 66

BEADLAM, Yorks

SE 6384   4th cent   f 1966

Covered over in situ

The mosaics in this villa are the most northerly yet known in Britain. Fragments of one floor, with borders of stepped traingles, guilloche and swastika pattern, were uncovered.

Illustrations The Ryedale Historian 3 (April 1967) 10 & JRS LVII (1967)179

BIGNOR, Sussex

SU 9814   4th cent   f 1811

A large and wealthy courtyard villa, first found in 1811, was excavated over a period of eight years. In 1814 huts were built to protect the best mosaics, whilst the remainder were covered over again after careful plans had been made. All the mosaics are fully illustrated in *Reliquiae Britannico Romanae III* (1817) by Samuel Lysons and those of which only fragments remained were convincingly reconstructed in the drawings.

a. (Room 3)   On view in situ (Site Museum)   plate 10B

A large room has a well restored apse bordered by an attractive floral scroll springing from a fluted urn. A medallion framing the nimbed bust of Venus is flanked by cornucopiae and peacocks perched on beribboned leaf sprays. The apse is linked to the rest of the mosaic floor by a narrow frieze of cupids dressed as gladiators, being instructed in the art of combat by cupid trainers.

23

The badly damaged square mosaic has a large octagon subdivided into eight small rectangular panels, containing dancing cupids, set round a large central octagon with contents destroyed. The spaces between these cupids are filled with a variety of interesting devices, flowers and cornucopiae. Two corners of the room hold an eight-petalled flower flanked by cornucopiae and two a fluted urn filled with fruit, foliate scrolls flowing from the sides.

Illustrations Lysons III (1817) pl XVI & Toynbee (1964) pl LIX b

b. (Room 6)   On view in situ (Site Museum)
A rectangular mosaic is divided into two squares by a central panel framing a squat urn, from which droop tendrils with leaves and flowers. Both squares have a central stylised flower set in perspective boxes decorated with various devices including swastikas and duplex knots.

Illustrations Lysons III (1817) pl XII & Morgan (1886) facing 204

c. (Room 7)
A large room is divided by short walls into two unequal sized rectangles. In the smaller, two narrow panels of decorated lozenges, enclosing a central duplex knot, flank a square holding a large circle with a castellated inner border and an outer border of cog-wheel triangles. In the centre, Zeus in the guise of a large eagle carries off Ganymede, who is wearing a cloak and a red Phrygian cap. In the spandrels are squat urns with small leaf sprays.

The larger part of the room has in the centre a hexagonal water basin from which radiate six hexagons with castellated borders, each framing a plump dancing girl, naked apart from whirling draperies. In triangular panels between the hexagons are eight-petalled flowers and leaves, the whole is contained by a large guilloche circle within a border of double swastikas. The spandrels hold urns and ivy leaf and lotus bud scrolls.

Illustrations Lysons III (1817) pl V & Toynbee (1963) pl 224

d. (Room 8)   On view in situ (Site Museum)
A floor of coarse red tesserae has a central mosaic 'mat', of which only the edges remain, but it was reconstructed in Lysons' drawing to show four simple saltires, each with a central guilloche bordered square framing a stylised flower.

Illustration Lysons III (1817) pl XI

e. (North Corridor 10)   On view in situ (Site Museum)
A broad guilloche bordered panel with plain black swastikas enclosing red hollow squares, each framing a small red cross.

Illustrations Lysons III (1817) pl X & Smith, D J (1969) pl 4.2

f. (Room 26)   Fragments on view in situ (Site Museum)
A large room with a hypocaust was unfortunately very badly damaged. According to Lysons' reconstruction drawing it had been divided into

two squares by a panel of floral scroll, probably flowing from a central urn. One square had four sets of interlaced guilloche squares round a large central octagon, contents destroyed. The only surviving panel within the squares has a grim-faced and hooded bust of Winter holding a bare twig. Other panels frame eight-pointed stars, squat urns with drooping leaves and lozenges with various geometric devices including a small labyrinth. A panel along one side has a scroll of guilloche bordered circles framing duplex knots and flowers. The second square has a large guilloche bordered circle holding eight small hexagons round a large central octagon, all with contents destroyed. Each spandrel contains an oval guilloche bordered medallion, one framing a man, naked apart from his cloak. Variously shaped panels hold dolphins and pheasants perched on overflowing cornucopiae and one small panel has the letters 'TR', perhaps an abbreviation of the signature of the mosaicist.
Illustrations Lysons III (1817) pl XIII & Toynbee (1963) pl 218
g. (Room 33)   On view in situ (Site Museum)
Very little now remains of this poorly executed mosaic, which forms a small square mat at the foot of steps leading to the west corridor. A contemporary drawing shows a circle with an outer border of swastikas enclosing birds, fish and dolphins. A central roundel, bordered by a crude ivy leaf scroll, frames a head of Medusa and in the spandrels are busts of the Seasons.
Illustrations Lysons III (1817) pl XXIV & Smith, D J (1969) pl 4.2
h. (Room 55)   Illustration in Site Museum
When the bath suite was uncovered a floor of black and white chequers was found.
Illustration Lysons III (1817) pl XXIX
i. (Room 56)   Fragments on view in situ (Site Museum) Plate 13A
Four pairs of interlaced guilloche squares hold medallions with borders of wave crests, guilloche and stepped triangles framing stylised flowers. Round the sides are semi-circles with segmented flowers and in each corner a quarter-circle, all with the same borders as the above. A central medallion frames a fierce head of Medusa. The general design of the mosaic is identical to one probably found in The Avenue, Cirencester and very similar to others found at North Leigh, Oxfordshire and Bramdean, Hampshire.
Illustrations Lysons III (1817) pl XXVIII & Toynbee (1963) pl 224

BISHOPSTONE, Herefordshire
SO 4143   f 1812   Lost (?)

The selection of a good site for the building of a new parsonage near Kenchester in 1812 led to the discovery of a large and complex geometric pavement, apparently belonging to an important villa.

The mosaic has an all-over saltire design, the arms of the crosses decorated with a variety of devices, including peltae with tendrils, lotus urns with leaves, stylised flowers, swastikas and ivy leaves etc. Of the central medallions, two hold an urn with leaves and tendrils and two a duplex knot in a sixteen-petalled 'sunflower'. Superimposed on this design is a large central diamond holding interlaced guilloche squares round a medallion with contents destroyed. In each of two corners is an urn with unusual handles and, in two, a pair of lotus flowers with convoluted petals. The outer border is of swastikas enclosing panels of guilloche and 'Z' patterns and the inner border has an unusual scroll, apparently composed of a series of cornucopiae with convoluted stems.

Illustration VCH Herefordshire I (1908) fig 14

BOX, Wilts

ST 8268   Coloured drawings in Devizes Museum

A large villa of some forty rooms, many of them with mosaic floors, was excavated between 1831 and 1902.

a. (Corridor I)   Covered over in situ
An all-over peltae pattern.
Illustrations WAM XXXIII (1904) 245 and 344 fig 2

b. (Corridor IV)
A strip of large blue swastikas on a white ground.
Illustration WAM XXXIII (1904) 247

c. (Room VI)   Covered over in situ
A large square mosaic has perspective boxes decorated with a great variety of devices, including lozenge swastikas, guilloche mats, flowers and small diamonds and triangles, and framing two central interlaced guilloche squares and four guilloche bordered medallions containing large stylised flowers. Along one side runs an unusual leafless floral scroll, similar to the border of Room 10 at Woodchester, Gloucestershire, and an outer border of widely spaced 'Z' patterns.
Illustration WAM XXXIII (1904) 248 and 344

d. (Room VIII)
A large duplex knot in a square panel surrounded by swastika pattern.
Illustration WAM XXXIII (1904) 249

e. (Corridor IX)
Large tesserae in alternate squares of buff and chocolate brown.
Reference WAM XXXIII (1904) 250

f. (Room XX)
A 'mat' of involved all-over swastika pattern.
Illustration WAM XXXIII (1904) 344 fig 1

BOXMOOR (Hemel Hempstead), Herts
SP 0305   2nd cent (?)   Lost

Re-excavation of this villa site in 1966 revealed that one mosaic found in 1851 had been totally destroyed and of two others only small fragments survived.
Illustration Britannia I (1970) pl XVA
Room 3   f 1851
An all-over pattern of swastikas in black on a white ground, the arms forming lozenges and framing a central square panel with contents destroyed. Set round this are four guilloche-bordered medallions, one holding a graceful urn. Various other panels frame pelta-duplex-swastikas, small peltae, flowers, leaves and two lotus urns.
Illustration VCH Hertfordshire IV (1914) pl XII

BRADING, IOW
SZ 6086   4th cent   f 1880   On view in situ (Site Museum)

The owner of this large villa, beautifully situated in a combe leading to the sea, must have been a man of some learning, judging by the obscure symbolism of his mosaics.
a. (Corridor 6)
A coarse chequered floor is the setting for a square panel with guilloche-bordered medallion framing a particularly charming rendering of Orpheus. He is portrayed as the dominating figure, seated in the centre, playing his lyre to a red-capped monkey, a small fox, a chough(?) and a pheasant, all apparently mesmerised by his music. In the one surviving spandrel is a bust with a bare twig, probably Winter, all executed in simple black outline
Illustration VCH Hampshire I (1900) fig 22
b. (Room 2)
The most obscure and intriguing of the mosaics is divided into a grid of panels by small red and white chequers, which also border a central medallion framing a long-haired naked bust, with a rod held over the right shoulder. Of three surviving panels, one contains a little house on a hill reached by steps or a ladder, flanked by a pair of griffins facing in opposite directions, and a figure with a cock's head and feet and a human body, possibly the gnostic Abraxes. The next panel shows two gladiators fighting and the third a red fox slinking past a tree towards a domed hut with a cross (?) at its apex. The only surviving corner holds a quarter-circle with another naked bust holding a rod, here topped by a minute cross. The small figured part of the mosaic is set in coarse black and white chequers.
Illustration VCH Hampshire I (1900) fig 22
c. (Room 9)

27

A square set in a wide border of coarse tesserae holds a plain diamond framing a small medallion.
Illustration VCH Hampshire I (1900) fig 21 (plan)
d. (Room 12)
The principal room is divided by two short walls, the larger mosaic being badly damaged but enough having survived to show a grid pattern with mythological scenes. A central medallion may have held a head of Medusa, which is also figured in one rectangular panel where Perseus triumphantly shows the severed head of Medusa to Andromeda. The remaining three rectangular panels hold fragments of figures and probably the roof of a house. Each corner square has one of the Seasons framed in guilloche and a peacock with fruits and flowers. In the surrounding coarse tessellation is a border of 'T' shapes and, prominently placed at the end of the room, a swastika framed in a semi-circle.

In a panel between the two short walls an astronomer points with his rod to a globe, a sundial on a pedestal is on his right and a bowl on his left. This scene is flanked by two rectangles, each with a lozenge framing a medallion, similar to the central design in Room 9.

The mosaic in the smaller room has five square panels forming a cross, with a central medallion framing yet another Medusa, and on the arms of the cross are:-
i. The mad Lycurgus, vine leaves sprouting from his own body, brandishing an axe at the frightened Maenad, Ambrosia.
ii. A Satyr chasing a coyly retreating Maenad.
iii. Ceres presenting Triptolemus with a sheaf of corn and a ploughshare.
iv. A shepherd with crook and pipes making advances to a Maenad, who dances to the music of her tambourine.

Triangles between the arms of the cross hold Wind gods with wings in their hair, blowing on slender conch shells, as at Frampton, Dorset and Pitney, Somerset.

In a long narrow panel at one end of the room Triton (?), holding an oar and a bowl, is flanked by Nereids riding on Sea Centaurs.
Illustration VCH Hampshire I (1900) fig 23

BRAMDEAN, Hants
SU 6228   4th cent   f 1832   Lost

Sampler in City Museum, Winchester
A large villa, only partially excavated, had a number of red tessellated floors and two mosaics of great interest.
a. A square pavement has a central guilloche bordered medallion from which radiate guilloche 'spokes' forming eight flat-topped triangular panels. In the centre, interlaced squares hold a head of Medusa and the six surviving panels contain gods of the week, starting with Sunday; Sol, Luna, Mars, Mercury, Jupiter and Venus. Saturn and the eighth bust, which may have

been Bonus Eventus or Fortuna, are missing. In each corner is a tiny urn.
Illustration VCH Hampshire I (1900) fig 18

b. plate 2A

Four unidentifiable busts are each heavily framed by four sets of two pairs
of interlaced guilloche squares, one within the other, the outer pairs forming a central octagon which holds one of the Labours of Hercules. The
giant Antaeus is being crushed to death by Hercules, who has lifted him off
the earth from which he derived his strength. Minerva, in crested helmet,
sits watching and encouraging Hercules, whose club and lion's skin are laid
to one side.

In semi-circles round the edge are two pairs of dolphins and two urns
with tendril handles, and in two of the corners are rounded urns without
a base. The border of the mosaic is castellated.
Illustration VCH Hampshire I (1900) fig 19

BRANTINGHAM, Yorks
SE 9328   4th cent

The two pavements, found on this villa site north of the Humber estuary in
1941, lay within 100 yards of a later discovery in 1962 and probably all
formed part of a large courtyard building.

a. f 1941   Lost

A square containing a large medallion with an eight-pointed star or
circular fan.
Illustration YAJ XXXVII (1948-51) fig II

b. f 1941   In the Archaeology Museum, Hull

An unusual and most effective geometric design with a wide border of
shaded scale pattern enclosing a square of peltae, which are arranged in
pairs and executed in simple outline.
Illustration YAJ XXXVII (1948-51) fig IV

c. F 1962   In the Archaeology Museum Hull   plate 3B

A large and beautiful mosaic, artistically designed and skilfully executed
in subtle colours, far more classical in style than any other pavement in
Yorkshire. Within borders of decorated diamonds and interlaced circles is
a large square, intricately divided into variously shaped panels. A central
octagon with a red ground holds the nimbed head of a goddess wearing a
mural crown. Radiating from the sides of the octagon are eight panels each
containing a large round-bellied urn. Between the urns are eight large semi-
circles, each with a reclining female holding a spray of leaves, possibly
water nymphs, and in each corner is a large pelta with the central point
in the form of the foot of an urn. Flanking the square on two sides are
four guilloche bordered panels in the shape of niches and framing nimbed
goddesses, their hair done up in a top-knot. Between the niches are vari-

ously shaped urns, one with a lid (?) and another with sprays of leaves.
Illustrations JRS LIII (1963) pls XI and XII

BRATTON SEYMOUR, Somerset
ST 6629   3rd-4th cent   F 1968   Covered over in situ

When a road was constructed in 1834 Roman remains were found, and excavations in 1968 uncovered part of a villa and one damaged mosaic floor. The layout, which resembles that of the Yatton mosaic, consists of interlaced guilloche and 'Z' pattern squares holding a plain octagon, within which is a medallion with a border of key pattern very like one at Yarchester, Shropshire and probably also similar to a fragment from Glyde Path Road in Dorchester, Dorset. In the centre is a crudely executed bust, either with long straggling hair or wearing a hat or helmet and a garment adorned with a band of red triangles. A small animal or a bird appears to be sitting on the left shoulder. Enclosing the interlaced squares is a large circle of 'Z' pattern within a guilloche-bordered square, and in the one surviving spandrel is an ivy leaf with tendrils similar to one in a spandrel at Yarchester. There is an outer border of two-coloured right-angled triangles or bisected squares and within this, on two (?) sides a panel of clumsy lotus wreath very similar to the border of the mosaic in Old Broad Street in London.

This pavement is interesting, not only because it has motifs in common with several mosaics in other parts of the country, but because the geometric setting is well executed in comparison with the bust and the lotus wreath.
Reference JRS LVIII (1968)   No published illustration

BRENSCOMBE, Dorset
SY 9782   Covered over in situ

a. f 1961
A fragmentary border of brown and white triangles.
Illustration PDNHAS 85 (1963) fig 3
b. f 1967
A very small piece of sophisticated foliate scroll seen in a post hole appears to be very like the scroll found at Halstock.
Illustration RCHM photograph

BRISLINGTON, Somerset
ST 6170   f 1899

A corridor house with several mosaic and tessellated floors.
a. (Room 1)   On view in Kings Weston Site Museum
An effective all-over pattern of twelve small rectangles holding four-petalled flowers and duplex knots, interspersed with six diamonds

framing lotus urns, and between these panels are small twists of guilloche.
On one side only, there is a panel of chequers.
Illustrations TBGAS XXIII (1900) pls II and IV

b. (Room 2)   Central panel in Bristol City Museum
An unusual and attractive mosaic with a fluted urn set in a central square
bordered by wave crests and surrounded by four cushion-shaped panels,
each framing a four-petalled flower. On each side of the square is a small
rectangular panel with a dolphin; the ground of the remainder of the pavement is filled, symmetrically, with peltae, lotus flowers and ivy leaf tendrils.
Two sides have borders of rectangles and two of double swastika pattern.
Illustrations TBGAS XXIII (1900) pls V and VI

c. (Corridor)   Lost
Fragments show an arrangement of perspective boxes, each decorated with
four small ovals or shaded chequers.
Illustration TBGAS XXIII (1900) pl VII

BROMHAM, Wilts
ST 9765   f 1810

A corridor-type villa, with two adjacent pavements lying on different levels,
was excavated several times from 1810 onwards.

a. A square mosaic with two interlaced squares, one of guilloche and the
other of stepped triangles, framing a central medallion with contents
destroyed. In the one surviving corner of the outer square is a fluted urn.

b. A scatter of sea-beasts, dolphins, fish and ivy leaves within a plain border.
Illustration Hoare (1819) 123

CAERLEON *(Isca)*, Mon
ST 3490

A legionary fortress, founded in circa AD 74, with fortifications enclosing
about 51 acres, was situated on a terrace commanding the valley of the
River Usk. Extramural buildings included a large amphitheatre, a small de-
pendent civilian settlement, mausolea and temples. Only a few mosaics have
been discovered, but the two excavated inside the fortress are quite different
from anything found so far in the rest of Britain.

1. f 1692   plate 4
A square with an all-over pattern of touching circles, over which run concentric wavy bands of light-coloured tesserae. Superimposed on this pattern
is a hollow square which forms the centre of a crude saltire, the arms of
which are decorated with strange objects resembling little chessmen. In each
semi-circle is a bird, probably a pheasant, and in each corner, a cup filled
with red wine.

31

CAERLEON

Illustrations Camden's Britannia (1695) 603 & Boon (1972) fig 40
2. f 1866   In the Legionary Museum of Caerleon
A mosaic found in the headquarters building in the centre of the fortress area
was so damaged that the central panel was lost, but enough remains to show
a striking labyrinth in black on white, bordered by a graceful foliate scroll
springing from two urns. Shading seems to suggest smilax tendrils, as in a
somewhat similar, but finer scroll at Silchester, Hampshire.
Illustration Boon (1972) fig 42
3. Backhall Street   1st cent   f 1877   To be exhibited in the Legionary
Museum of Caerleon
Fragments of a strange and unique mosaic were found in baths within the fortress in 1877. A square with plain coloured borders holds a large guilloche-
bordered circle framing another square; the inner square frames a tendril
scroll and a series of concentric wreaths, one with chequered borders braided
with leaves or ribbon, and another bound with ribbon is similar to a border
enclosing a sea-beast at Dyer Street in Cirencester, Gloucestershire. The one
surviving inner spandrel holds a lotus bud (?) with tendrils, and the outer
spandrel has an extraordinary device, probably the beribboned head of a
thyrsus, or a spear disguised as such.
Illustrations BBCS XIX (1962) pls 3 and 4 & Boon (1972) fig 47
4. Civilian Settlement   f 1955
A courtyard-type house had a simple mosaic floor composed of a grid of
sixteen large squares, with a diamond at each intersection.
Illustration Photograph in the National Museum of Wales, Cardiff
5. Pilbach   f circa 1862
A mosaic of simple swastika pattern was found, probably in a mausoleum,
about a mile west of the fortress.
Illustration Lee, J E Isca Silurum (1862) pl XXVI

CAERWENT *(Venta Silurum)*, Mon
ST 4690

This *civitas* capital was founded in circa AD 75 and covered 44 acres, with a
regular grid of streets forming twenty *insulae*. Tessellated pavements were
first recorded in 1586 and several more were discovered and lost or destroyed
in the 17th and 18th centuries.
   Systematic annual excavations were carried out from 1899 to 1913, but
the *insulae* were not given numbers, so that the numbering of the buildings is
according to whether they lie north or south of the main east-west street
from Chepstow to Newport.
1. f 1689   Lost
Three pavements were found in Francis Ridley's garden, 'In one of these pavements, as the owner relates, were delineated several flowers, which he

1A (*above*) Holcombe, Devon. Geometric with urn-like lotus bud. (From coloured
drawing in the Society of Antiquaries of London)
1B (*below*) Grateley, Hampshire. Geometric with circular fan. (Coloured
engraving in Salisbury & South Wiltshire Museum)

2A
(*left*) Bramdean, Hampshire. Hercules and Antaeus. (From coloured engraving 1839, in Society of Antiquaries of London)

2B
(*below*) Fullerton, Hampshire. Virtus or Mars. (Drawing by David S. Neal)

DAVID S. NEAL, 1964

FULLERTON MANOR, WHERWELL, HANTS

SCALE

compared to Roses, Tulips, and Flowers-de-Luce; and at each of the four corners, a Crown, and a Peacock holding a Snake in his Bill, and treading it under one foot. Another had the figure of a Man in armour from the breast upward. There were also Imperial Heads, and some other variety of Figures . . .'
Reference Camden's Britannia (1695) 603

2. f 1763

'In an orchard adjoining the street was discovered, some few years ago, the remnant of a tessellated pavement, about a yard over; the colours are lively enough, but the figure of a dog, or other animal, under a tree very ill-expressed.'
Reference Arch II (1773) 3

3. f 1775

'Another pavement . . . was in a cellar or outhouse in an orchard belonging to Mrs Williams, on which was still preserved part of a vase and a bird, and on which there had been figures of a lion, a tiger, and a stag.' The 'vase' seems very unusual, with no foot and no handles.
Illustration Arch V (1779) pl I

4. f 1777   Lost

Adjacent to the bath block of a house in the south-east corner of the town, an ornate mosaic was found. Guilloche swastikas form thirteen octagons, twelve of which enclose medallions framing various stylised flowers. A panel with a heavy grid of squares, enclosing little crosses, lies on one side and the whole mosaic has a plain meander pattern border.
Illustration Arch XXXVI (1856) pl XXXIV

5. (Corridor 7)   4th cent   f 1855   In the National Museum of Wales, Cardiff

A corridor mosaic, found in the south-east corner, near the above, has four square panels, two with duplex knots in a medallion and two with a small guilloche mat.
Illustration Arch XXXVI (1856) pl XXXV

6. f 1886   Lost

Two mosaic pavements were found in the orchard behind the Coach and Horses Inn.

a. Although badly damaged by tree roots, enough remained to show a large octagon filling a guilloche bordered square and enclosing a central panel, contents destroyed, and large perspective boxes decorated with dolphins and pairs of leaves. A guilloche bordered square in each outer corner frames a quarter of a stylised flower, and there is a crude foliate scroll along one side of the pavement.
   Illustration Drawing in Newport Museum   Reference PSAL XI (1886) 195

b. A corridor of guilloche mat in four colours.

Illustration Drawing in Newport Museum
7. f 1893
A large house was found, on the corner immediately west of Pound Lane and north of the Newport to Chepstow road, prior to the construction of cottages on the site. It had a long tessellated corridor and several mosaics, of which one was destroyed, one had a border of meander pattern and of a third only a rather incoherent account and a small plan remain. A rectangular panel to one side of the room was said to resemble very closely a corridor mosaic found in Caerwent in 1855, and would therefore appear to have been divided into squares, with guilloche bordered medallions, triangles and duplex knots, and borders of 'key pattern', guilloche and blue and white triangles.
Reference PSAL XV (1894) 142
8. Building II N   f 1881   Lost
a. (Room 3)
A drawing of a fragmentary mosaic shows a large guilloche circle, within a square, divided by guilloche into eight hexagons round a central medallion, and on one side there was apparently a frieze of dolphins. A contemporary account stated 'that there had been four spandrils with a fish in each (a salmon) and eight hexagons each containing two fish; one of the hexagons had a trout, with an eel coiled up by the side of it.' This arrangement of hexagons was used twice at Bignor, Sussex, in one case surrounding a hexagonal basin.
Illustration Morgan, O Papers of the Monmouthshire & Caerleon
Antiquaries Association (1882) 22 Reference PSAL VIII (1881) 542
b. (Corridor 4)
The description of a fragment of black and white chequers, said to have been found here, may refer to the narrow rectangle and chequers in blue and red on a white ground shown in the illustration of Room 3.
Reference PSAL VIII (1881) 542
9. Building XXVII N (Room 13)   2nd cent (?)   f 1947   Covered over in situ
In a courtyard house in Pound Lane an attractive, but badly damaged mosaic was discovered in 1947. A guilloche-bordered saltire has a central medallion framing a fluted urn with ivy leaves trailing from the handles, and the arms of the cross decorated with twists of guilloche. Semi-circles or circles between the arms, each hold a pleasing little dolphin, somewhat similar to those in the mosaic at High Wycombe in Buckinghamshire.
Illustrations Photograph in Dept of the Environment & Arch Camb
supplemental volume forthcoming.
10. Building II S   f 1901
A large courtyard house, found near the south-west corner of the town, had a number of very fragmentary mosaic floors with swastika pattern, a lotus

urn, ivy leaf and duplex knots among the designs.
Illustrations Drawings in Newport Museum & Arch LVIII (1902) pl VIII (plan)
11. Building VI S (Room 8)   f 1902
Only fragments of a large geometric mosaic survived, showing a border of bold meander pattern in black on a white ground.
Reference Arch LVIII (1903) 400
12. Building VII S   f 1901
a. (Room 6) Fragments stored in Newport Museum
   Borders of chequers, triangles and guilloche frame a large square of perspective boxes set round a badly damaged central medallion. It has been suggested that this could have contained Orpheus, but in view of the general design and the paucity of animals, it must remain a very tentative assumption. Four guilloche medallions hold curious little naked figures with wings or ribbons, two carrying a torch (?) and one a key-shaped object. Panels in the four corners hold busts of the Seasons, and on each side toy-like animals, including a lion and a hare.
   Illustration Arch LVIII (1902) pl X
b. (Room 7)   Fragment in Newport Museum
   i. An unusual geometric design with three borders of stepped triangles, decreasing in size towards the centre. Plain lines divide the mosaic into a grid containing squares, diamonds and circles, and the large central medallion has an interesting 'ruched' border.
   Illustration Arch LVIII (1902) pl XI
   ii. A later pavement, lying over the last, has perspective box pattern in black and white framing four 'L' shapes. The whole of the centre of the mosaic was destroyed.
   Illustration Arch LVIII (1902) pl VIII (plan)
13. Building XI S
(Room 8)   f 1904
A long mosaic panel has alternate squares of guilloche mat and swastika pattern.
Illustration Drawing in Newport Museum   Reference Arch LIX (1905) 295
14. Building XII S   f 1904
A large courtyard building, lying close to the wall near the south gate, had a number of tessellated floors and badly damaged mosaics.
a. (Room 17)
   A fragmentary square of perspective boxes decorated with duplex knots and segmented flowers. The guilloche border forms a large meander on at least one side of the mosaic.
   Illustration Drawing in Newport Museum   Reference Arch LIX (1905) 301
b. (Room 18)

37

A square containing a large guilloche-bordered circle, contents destroyed, and a segmented stylised flower in each spandrel.
Illustration Drawing in Newport Museum *Reference Arch LIX (1905) 301*
c. (Room 29)
A fragment shows a border of squares and 'L' shapes, and a piece of geometric pattern with guilloche and lozenges.
Illustration Drawing in Newport Museum *Ref Arch LIX (1905) 304*
d. (Room 36) 2nd cent
A large room with a gently curved apse, has a mosaic with some unusual features. The main area of the room has an all-over pattern of perspective boxes with curved sides, framing stylised flowers. Between two borders of triangles is a crude bead-and-reel pattern, and the apse is filled with bands of triangles and diamonds and three rows of bisected circles.
Illustrations Arch LIX (1905) pl LXVIII & photograph in Newport Museum

CALNE (Wans House), Wilts
ST 9667 f 1765

In 1796 it was reported that a pavement found here about thirty years before was still in good condition, covered with earth and thought to represent 'a Roman soldier, or military officer of higher rank, of the natural size, armed with a spear', but is more likely to have been the god Mars.
Reference Gents Mag 1796 i 472

CANTERBURY *(Durovernum Cantiacorum)*, Kent
TR 1457

Owing to its strategic position on a crossing of the River Stour, where roads from Dover, Lympe, Richborough and London converged, a town of some 130 acres grew up and probably became a *civitas* capital. Due to a considerable rise in the level of the ground and to uninterrupted occupation of the site, very few mosaics have so far been discovered.
1. Burgate Street f 1868 In Roman Pavement Museum, Canterbury
Discoveries on this site included several plain tessellated floors and a fragment of mosaic with a medallion framing a crudely executed urn.
Illustration Morgan (1886) facing 154
2. Butchery Lane f 1946 In Roman Pavement Museum, Canterbury
Building II (Room 2)
Spaced out along a tessellated corridor were three rectangular mosaic 'mats' with guilloche borders. The central panel has a large stylised flower and two inner borders of diamonds. The other two have a stylised flower set in a diamond with an ivy leaf in each corner and two inner borders of the unusual dog's-tooth triangles.

Illustrations Frere, S S Roman Canterbury (1962) cover & Arch Cant LXI (1948) pl I
3. High Street (County Hotel)   f 1758   Lost
A drawing shows a fragment with an unusual design. In the centre a guilloche 'archway' holds an entrance with two columns flanked by two disproportionately large stylised flowers, each in a guilloche bordered square.
Illustration Gents Mag 1805 i pl II

CARISBROOKE, IOW
SZ 4888   f 1859   In situ
A villa with tessellated and mosaic floors was found in the vicarage garden.
a. (Room D)   Drawing in Carisbrooke Castle Museum
  A rectangular pavement is divided by short panels of guilloche and small chequers into nine compartments. The largest, in the centre, frames an attractive urn arranged with sprays of leaves, and round the edges are panels of lotus flowers and ivy leaves, one of which is flanked by two leafy twigs.
  Illustration VCH Hampshire I (1900) fig 26
b. (Room H)
  The largest floor in the villa has a mosaic of plain red and white chequers.
  Illustration VCH Hampshire I (1900) fig 25 (plan)

CASTOR, Northants

Castor village and nearby Mill Hill both seem to have been the site of large villas, probably belonging to rich industrialists concerned with the thriving potteries situated in the valley of the River Nene. E T Artis excavated both sites in the early 19th century, but unfortunately left little record apart from a series of coloured drawings from which the following mosaics have been described.
1. Mill Hill   TL 1297
a. f 1822
  A fluted urn with no handles stands on a plinth, framed in a loop of guilloche within an octagon formed by eight panels of geometric pattern, which also serve as decoration for perspective boxes in the surrounding square. An attractive arrangement of small black, white and red chequers is interspersed with four square panels framing pelta-duplex-swastikas and guilloche mat. This decorative 'rug' lies on a ground of large chequers executed in coarse tesserae.
  Illustrations Artis (1828) pls XVIII and XIX
b. f 1822
  A simple all-over pattern of large interlaced circles. According to Artis, these two pavements came from the same house.

39

Illustrations Artis (1828) pl XXI & VCH Northamptonshire I (1902) 172

c. f 1822

A small oblong building with an apsed corridor had a simple floor with large chequers.

Illustration Artis (1828) pl XX (plan)

d. f 1822

Again according to Artis, another small building had one room and a corridor similarly paved with chequers.

Illustration Artis (1828) pl XXII (plan)

2. Village   TL 1298

a. f 1827

A series of concentric rectangles with the central panel divided into two 'L' shapes.

Illustration Artis (1828) pl VII

b. f 1821   In the old dairy at Milton Hall

A circle within a square frames a stylised flower with eight large heart-shaped petals, and an outer ring of pointed petals forming semi-circles round the circumference of the enclosing circle. The spandrels hold small lotus buds and lotus urns, and a broad border is decorated with lozenges, duplex knots, hearts and minute peltae with tendrils.

Illustration Artis (1828) pl XII

c. f 1821

A very curious mosaic with a large area of guilloche mat holding a series of concentric rectangles, which frame a blank central panel. There is also a blank central square on a striped ground at Greetwell Fields, Lincoln.

Illustration Artis (1828) pls III and IV

CHEDWORTH, Glos

SP 0513   4th cent   f 1864   On view in situ   (Site Museum)

A villa, lying beside a spring in a beautiful woodland setting, has been ex-cavated several times between 1864 and 1964. There were a number of mosaics, but many have been lost and some covered over in situ. Those which may now be seen lie in the dining-room and the two bath suites.

a. (Room 5)

The dining-room is divided by slightly projecting walls and of the two mosaics the first, and more interesting, is badly damaged. It is composed of a large octagon with a simple scroll border and a small central octagon, now lost, from which radiate eight flat-topped triangular panels containing Satyrs and Maenads. In each of the four outer corners is a small boy or cupid representing one of the Seasons, the most attractive being Winter, heavily clad and carrying a dead hare and a bare twig. The layout resembles that of a mosaic at Pitney in Somerset.

The mosaic in the other part of the room has an all-over guilloche swastika pattern enclosing squares of guilloche mat and a central pelta-duplex-swastika. Panels on two sides each have a heavy acanthus leaf scroll springing from a central urn.
Illustration Durant, G M Journey into Roman Britain (1960) 217

b. (Room 10)

A large guilloche bordered saltire has an urn in the central roundel and the arms of the cross decorated with convoluted pelta urns. Between the arms are triangles, two framing water lilies and one a pigeon pecking at a flower.
Illustration Ant J XLIX (1969) pl XXXIXb

c. (Room 11)

An all-over pattern of shaded interlaced circles forming quatrefoils.
Illustration JBAA XXIV (1868) pl 10

d. (Room 14)

An unusual and attractive peltae pattern, the peltae being placed tip to tip, thus forming circles which are divided into small red and white triangles.
Illustration JBAA XXIV (1868) pl 10

e. A narrow passage leading to Room 14 had a badly damaged mosaic of swastika pattern enclosing guilloche bordered square panels.
Illustration Drawing by Fox, G E in Society of Antiquaries of London

CHERHILL, Wilts

SU 0370   4th cent (?)   f 1913   Covered over in situ

A well preserved fragment, re-excavated and photographed in 1938, shows a large hound or some wild animal bounding past a tree, its heavy forequarters suggesting a lion but the smooth pointed tail, a dog.
Illustration Blackford, J H Cherhill (1941) 32

CHESTER *(Deva)*, Cheshire

SJ 4066

A Legionary fortress with defences enclosing nearly 60 acres has so far pro-duced mosaic pavements on only one site.

St. Michael's Arcade (Bridge Street)

Part of the internal bath building was first found in the 18th century and subsequent excavations have uncovered hypocausts and some simple but strange mosaics.

a. (Watergate)   f 1779

A pavement over a hypocaust, executed in three colours 'ran in a circular Mosaic figure' and was the only one in Chester to have colours other than black and white. *Reference Watkin (1886) 155*

b. (Room B)   f 1863

A fragment over a hypocaust shows part of a large circle cut by eight spokes which radiate from a central octagon enclosing a black medallion, the whole executed in plain black lines on a white ground.
Illustration Watkin (1886) facing 134 (plan)
c. (Room C)   f 1863
A rectangular pavement with white transverse stripes on a black ground.
Illustration Watkin (1886) facing 134 (plan)
d. (Room D)   f 1863
A very interesting fragment of mosaic in an apse (?) has a line of five triangles lying next to a bottle-shaped figure, topped by a circle with four irregular spokes, all outlined in black on a white ground. This may be the symbol of the punic (Carthaginian) goddess Tanit, usually shown with transverse lines like arms, or the sign of the 'bottle', also indicative of the worship of Tanit.
Illustration Watkin (1886) facing 134 (plan)
e. f 1909   Fragments in cellars of St Michael's Arcade
A large, badly damaged floor has two big black and white striped dolphins and part of another sea-beast in black, and a border of white squares set in the black surround. A fragment shows an extension of the black ground with a square cut across the corners to form an octagon enclosing a black square holding concentric diamonds, the whole executed in plain black lines on a white ground.
Illustration Thompson, F H Roman Cheshire (1965) frontispiece

CHESTERS (Woolaston), Glos
ST 5998   f 1933(?)   Fragments stored in City Museum, Gloucester

Attributed to this site is a fragment of mosaic showing a fluted urn, said to have been found thrown into a bath.
Illustration TBGAS LXXXVI (1967) pl XXIII

CHESTERTON (The Castles, Water Newton) *(Durobrivae)*, Hunts
TL 1297

The site of the town of *Durobrivae*, also known as 'The Castles', is a fortified hexagon of some 45 acres straddling Ermine Street between Chesterton and Water Newton. It may have been the centre of the important Nene Valley pottery industry, and it was certainly the centre of a complex of buildings and potteries. It is also thought to have been the site of the workshop of the Durobrivan school of mosaicists, a theory partially based on the discovery by Artis of a heap of sorted tesserae in a building in the town.
1. f circa 1820
According to Artis, a 'strong building' had white tesserae lining the lower

part of the walls of a room.
Illustration Artis (1828) pl XXVI
2. f 1858   In Orton Hall School
An all-over pattern of shaded interlaced circles with a four-petalled flower in the centre of each circle.
Illustration RCHM Huntingdonshire (1926) pl 2

CHICHESTER *(Noviomagus Regentium)*, Sussex
SU 8604

A *civitas* capital and port with fortifications enclosing over 100 acres.
1. **Cathedral**
A number of red tessellated pavements were found here in the 19th century, and in 1966 two mosaics were discovered behind the altar in the south aisle.
a. (Room 1)   On view in situ
   A fragment of black swastika pattern enclosing a stylised flower.
   Illustration Down & Rule (1971) pls 6 and 13
b. (Room 6)
   A small fragment of swastika pattern enclosing squares in red on a grey ground.
   Illustration Down & Rule (1971) pl 7
2. **East Street** (David Greig's shop)   3rd cent (?)   f 1959
   Fragments in City Museum, Guildhall, Chichester
Interesting fragments show a border of foliate scroll and square panels, framing stylised flowers, one with the dog's tooth border, a motif which may also be found at Butchery Lane in Canterbury, Kent. Smaller squares are decorated with interlaced circles forming quatrefoils, and with pelta-duplex-swastikas. This is possibly part of an all-over pattern of squares and diamonds similar to the mosaic found at 45 North Hill, Colchester, Essex.
No published illustration   Reference Down & Rule (1971) 10
3. **West Street** (Morant's shop)   f 1960   In situ
A fragment of black and white mosaic from a bath block has a pattern of decorated perspective boxes forming stars and framing a chequered square.
Illustration Holmes, J Chichester - The Roman Town (Chichester 1965) fig 6

CHILGROVE, Sussex

1. **Cross Roads Field**   SU 8413   4th cent (?)   f 1966   Covered over in situ
Two distinct but contiguous buildings both had mosaics, one in the main villa had been destroyed by ploughing but the second, in the aisled barn, was a remarkable pavement, probably unique in the Roman Empire. A plain tessellated floor has a series of nine circles, 18 inches in diameter, executed in red

and white. Seven are in a line running approximately north to south, while the other two lie parallel at the other side of the room. The patterns are all different and include various arrangements of concentric circles and a plain circle round a small central cross. It is possible that this was used for some game, as may also have been the Corridor in Insula 1.2 at Silchester in Hampshire.

Illustration JRS LVII (1967) pl XV.2

2. Brick Kiln Farm   SU 8312   4th cent   f 1964   Raised and awaiting restoration

A long rectangular building with heated rooms and mosaic pavements was bounded by a ditch. An attractive square mosaic has a large guilloche-bordered octagon enclosing interlaced guilloche squares and a central medallion with contents destroyed. Lozenges within the octagon frame leaf motifs, and the two surviving outer corners hold urn-like lotus buds with winding tendrils.

Illustration In forthcoming Sussex Archaeological Trust publication

CIRENCESTER *(Corinium Dobunnorum)*, **Glos**
SP 0201

A *civitas,* and eventually a provincial capital of some 240 acres, second only in size to London, which probably owed its wealth and importance to the flourishing state of agriculture in that area. It was endowed with wide colonnaded streets, public buildings and rich houses, their floors paved with sophisticated mosaics. A number of these, beautifully preserved, can be seen in the Corinium Museum in Cirencester, together with fragments showing an urn in a roundel, set in perspective boxes decorated with duplex knots and guilloche, and a rectangular panel of lotus-bud and ivy-leaf scroll, all thought to have come from the Ashcroft area in the early 20th century.

1. Ashcroft Road (Ashcroft House) (Insula XX.2)   f 1964
a. Fragment in Corinium Museum

    A white band, with rows of four octagons outlined in black, each enclosing a small red cross, runs the length of a red tessellated corridor.

    Illustration Ant J XLV (1965) pl XXXIIIa

b. 4th cent

    One border of this badly damaged mosaic lay over the corridor, which was of an earlier date. A variety of wide borders and panels of swastikas, chequers, peltae and shaded interlaced circles forming quatrefoils, cover most of the floor and frame a square. A heavy saltire in the centre has the arms decorated with lozenges, duplex knots, ivy leaves and at least one fluted urn, which appears to be very similar to that found in Beeches Road and to the urn-like lotus flower at Holcombe in Devon. The central medallion frames a duplex knot backed by peltae with tendrils and leaves, and triangles between the arms of the cross hold segmented stylised flowers.

Illustration Ant J XLV (1965) pl XXXIIIa

c. 4th cent

A rather unusual asymmetric mosaic 'rug' set in wide bands of coarse tesserae was partially uncovered. An octagon, bordered by a lotus wreath, frames a stylised flower, variously shaped panels hold a variety of leaves, flowers, duplex knots and twists of guilloche, and one has a border of looped ribbon. The general effect is similar to that of a fragmentary mosaic found at Woolstone in Berkshire, the looped ribbon resembles the inner border at Whitton in Suffolk and the lotus wreath is like the border of an octagon in Blackfriars Street, Leicester.

Illustration Ant J XLV (1965) pl XXXIIIb

2. Ashcroft Road (Brewery Car Park)   2nd cent(?)   f 1961

Stored in the Mycalex factory, Cirencester

A simple guilloche grid pattern with a stylised flower in each corner square, guilloche lozenges in two of the rectangular panels, and in each of the others a guilloche mat. The central guilloche bordered medallion frames a badly damaged urn.

Illustration Illustrated London News 2 December 1950 912

3. Ashcroft Villas   f 1902   Lost   plate 8A

A plunge bath with stone steps descending into it and a pavement were found in digging foundations for the houses known as Ashcroft Villas. A powerful head of Neptune, with wavy hair, green glass tesserae in his beard and a trident behind his head, is flanked by sea-beasts, fishes and dolphins.

Illustration Photographic plate in the Haverfield Collection, Ashmolean Museum, Oxford   Ref Arch LXIX (1917) 176 no 20

4. The Avenue (The Leauses)   f 1808   plate 13B

Samuel Lysons described a pavement as follows: 'In the year 1808, on some pasture ground . . . being broken up for garden ground, adjoining the Leweses garden . . . a mosaic pavement was discovered . . . in the general style of its ornaments much resembling the Bignor pavement, in the centre of which is the head of Minerva.'

There is a Lysons drawing of a mosaic found in Cirencester, which shows four interlaced guilloche squares, each forming an octagon and framing a stylised flower. A central medallion holds a four-petalled flower, and semi-circles along the sides have segmented stylised flowers; in the four corners are ivy leaves and lotus buds. The design of this mosaic is identical to that of the Medusa mosaic at Bignor, Sussex, which leads me to the conclusion that this must be an illustration of the floor described above.

Illustration Lysons II (1817) pl V Reference Lysons III (1817) 10

5. The Avenue (Insula I)   4th cent   f 1963

A colonnade in the Forum had a series of simple geometric patterns, some of them very reminiscent of the black and white 1st century mosaics at Fishbourne in Sussex. The fragments show panels with brick pattern in outline, a grid of squares containing chequers and small black squares, and chequers in three colours set diagonally.

Illustration Ant J XLIV (1964) pl XIIb

6. The Avenue (Insula XIV.2)   f 1968   Covered over in situ

Excavations revealed a house with 4th century mosaics overlying at least one which is probably of the 2nd century.

a. (Room 4)

i   2nd cent (?)

A corner fragment with swastika pattern enclosing panels of guilloche and a small four-petalled flower. An outer border of blue bands may have been part of a large labyrinth pattern, as at Caerleon in Monmouthshire.

Illustration Ant J XLIX (1969) pls XXXVa and XXXVIIb

ii   4th cent   Raised and awaiting restoration

A fragmentary mosaic lying over the earlier pavement probably has an all-over pattern of saltires, the short arms decorated with pelta urns with convoluted handles. The one surviving central medallion frames a stylised flower, and a square of guilloche mat lies between the crosses.

Illustration Ant J XLIX (1969) pl XXXVIIIa

b. (Corridor 5)

Rectangles of swastika pattern alternate with squares of guilloche mat.

Illustration Ant J XLIX (1969) pl XXXVIIIb

c. (Corridor 10)

Adjacent panels of concentric rectangles in blue on white with a blue band in the centre of each panel. A very similar corridor mosaic was found in Dorchester Prison in Dorset.

Illustration Ant J XLIX (1969) pl XXXIXa

7. Beeches Road (Insula XII)   f 1971

A well preserved town house with a bath suite and some very striking mosaic floors was discovered in 1971. An interim report will appear in the *Antiquaries Journal* in 1973.

a. Interlaced guilloche squares enclose a medallion with plain borders framing an attractive hare crouching among leafy plants, reminiscent of the hare among rocks (?) at Pitmeads in Wiltshire. The squares are set among perspective boxes decorated with shaded chequers, guilloche, triangles and stylised flowers, one of the latter being unique in Britain. A rectangular panel leading to another room has an unusual fluted urn with the neck formed like a lotus flower, very similar to the urn in Ashcroft Road b. above. On the leafy tendrils which trail from the handles are perched two pheasants.

Illustration Current Archaeology 29 (November 1971) 151

b. An adjacent square mosaic has a central medallion with contents destroyed, bordered by two concentric bands of guilloche. In the spandrels are tall fluted urns from which flow convoluted tendril scrolls.

Illustration Current Archaeology 29 (November 1971) 151

c. A rectangular panel of coarse swastikas enclosing squares with hourglass triangles and small cushion-shapes.

Illustration Current Archaeology 29 (November 1971) 149

d. A fragmentary mosaic with a fine swastika pattern may not belong to this house.

No published illustration

8. Dyer Court f 1957 Covered over in situ

A large building found here was only partially excavated.

a. A corridor with a double swastika pattern in black on white.

Illustration TBGAS LXXVIII (1959) fig 2

b. A small fragment of swastika and guilloche border and traces of the main design, which could have been a pattern of saltires or octagons.

Illustration TBGAS LXXVIII (1959) fig 3

9. Dyer Street f 1777 Lost

Part of a large square mosaic was taken up and laid in the garden of a Mr Croome, where it gradually deteriorated and was finally destroyed by the elements. Rudder described it in his book published in 1833: 'It had a chequered border round it . . . The pavement was divided into four equal compartments, by the artful arrangement and disposition of the different coloured materials, into lines of hearts linked together, or rather interlaced fretwise, which had a very pretty effect. There was a central piece, consisting of an octagon; and it had also a small figure of the same kind, in the middle of each compartment. All besides, within the borders and compartments, consisted of chequered-work, . . . much smaller than those of which the border consisted.'

A drawing by Lysons *(Reliquiae II pl V)* has been suggested as an illustration of this mosaic, but I do not think it tallies with Rudder's description, whereas it does appear to portray the mosaic found in The Avenue in 1808.

Reference Rudder (1833) 61

10. Dyer Street (Insula XVII) f 1783 Lost

In the street, near the pavements found in 1849, another even more sophisticated mosaic had been discovered in 1783, and was fortunately drawn by Lysons before it was destroyed. A scatter of marine figures on a white ground bears a greater resemblance to similar mosaics found in the Mediterranean area than anything so far discovered in Britain. The large fragment shows various sea-beasts, fishes, an eel, a shellfish, a shrimp, a crab, a jellyfish and dolphins carrying a Nereid and a Cupid, while another Cupid holds the wheel of a chariot, possibly bearing the god Neptune. The border is of blue double swastika pattern framing panels with quincunx and eight-petalled flowers. Recent re-excavation in the cellars of the present houses revealed an 8 inch strip of this pavement, which was enough to confirm the accuracy of Lysons' illustration.

Illustration Toynbee (1963) pl 213   Reference TBGAS LXXXIX (1970) 175

11.   Dyer Street   f after 1783

'Neptune with black and blue labyrinthine fret on white ground. Chequered border in black, yellow, red, white.'

Reference Arch LXIX (1917) 175 no 8b

12.   Dyer Street   4th cent (?)   f 1820   Lost

A mosaic, possibly belonging to the same house as those found in 1849, was seen, drawn and described by Beecham. The central medallion is dominated by an extraordinary little man brandishing a spear and an axe (?), his legs ending in curling fishes' tails, and with a third tail (?) between his legs. It is worth comparing this strange creature with Triton (?) at Brading on the Isle of Wight. Below him, scuttling fearfully away with his lyre, is Orpheus flanked by two dog-like animals. Concentric circular bands hold first a procession of birds, then three strings of oval beads or a wreath of leaves (?), next a procession of beasts and finally a plain meander pattern with a small band in each loop. Each spandrel holds a flower in a spray of leaves within a border of dog's tooth triangles. The borders of the mosaic are composed of narrow bands, one divided into little squares and rectangles, some holding a simple labyrinth pattern.

Illustrations Beecham (1886) 266 & Smith, D J (1965) fig 12

13.   Dyer Street (Insula XVII)   f 1849

A Roman house running obliquely across Dyer Street from the Ship Inn, had a number of very sophisticated mosaic pavements.

a. In Corinium Museum

A slightly damaged square mosaic, bordered by chequers, has a saltire with a large central roundel framing one big and two small dogs in hot pursuit of a now vanished quarry. The arms of the cross are asymmetrically decorated with two masks of Neptune, very similar to the one in the apse of the mosaic found in Fordington High Street, Dorchester in Dorset, a large stylised flower and a guilloche mat, bordered by small black peltae. Between the arms of the cross, one semi-circle holds a large winged sea-beast chasing a dolphin, while on the opposite side another, reduced in size by inner borders of dog's tooth triangles and 'T' shapes, frames a much smaller sea-beast, also chasing a dolphin. The third semi-circle has inner borders of rainbow shading (?) bound with ribbon, and little black semi-circles framing a small spray of ivy leaves. Two of the surviving corner panels hold geometric motifs and the third a head of Medusa, probably balanced by

another in the missing corner.
Illustration Buckman & Newmarch (1850) pl VI
b. In Corinium Museum   plate 12A
This very attractive mosaic is composed of nine octagons, two of which
were totally destroyed, but of those remaining, each frames a roundel. In
the centre, only the forelegs of a horse survive, but the stance and the
presence of the surrounding mythological figures suggest that it may have
been a Centaur. In the corner roundels are busts of the four Seasons,
Spring with flowers in her hair and a bird on her shoulder, Summer with
corn-ears and sickle and Autumn wearing a wreath of fruit and holding a
plough; Winter is lost. Between the four Seasons, the medallions hold the
old man Silenus reclining heavily on a rather mis-shapen donkey, Actaeon
being attacked by his dogs as he changes into a stag and a damaged roundel
framing a youthful Bacchus with a crown of vine leaves, a thyrsus and a
leopard skin. In two surviving small squares between the octagons are a
head of Medusa and a Bacchante.
Illustration Buckman & Newmarch (1850) pl II
c. A fragment of colourful foliate scroll appears to have been the floor of a
passage.
Illustration Buckman & Newmarch (1850) pl VI fig 2
14.   Querns Lane   f 1837   In a garden shed
A badly damaged mosaic, which could still be seen in a summer house in
1851, was said to have had guilloche borders and to have 'consisted of five
involved squares, so arranged as to form octagonal medallions, the centre of
the only perfect one being filled up by what is, perhaps, intended for a four-
petalled flower; this heart-shaped petalloid form is extremely common, either
single or in combination.'
Reference Buckman & Newmarch (1850) 32
15.   Victoria Road
a. 'The Firs'   f circa 1850   covered over in situ
'A floor with a bird in the centre' lies beneath the hall of a private house
and a large number of red tessellated pavements were discovered in the
garden in 1868.
Reference Arch LXIX (1917) 177 no 35
b. Bingham Hall   f 1929
In the garden of Bingham Hall, which was part of the original garden of
'The Firs' before King Street was made, a fragment of mosaic border was
re-excavated in 1958. The pattern is of great interest, being composed of
a pelta from which flow two convoluted floral scrolls. Between the 'feet'
of the pelta are two smaller peltae, each enclosing a heart; an identical
geometric device decorates a perspective box at Halstock in Dorset.
Illustration Drawing in Corinium Museum

49

16. Victoria Road 2nd cent (?)   f 1922   Covered over in situ (?)
Four mosaics belonging to a large house were uncovered by building operations, but no adequate record of the site was made. Interesting pattern.
a. An all-over pattern of black and white rectangles, squares and triangles
symmetrically arranged within plain borders of red and white.
Illustration JRS XI (1921) pl XIX
b. Fragments of a large floor show borders of guilloche and swastika
pattern. 'From this sprang, towards the inner area, or field, of the floor
a series of small semi-circles of key-border and guilloche . . . and in the
centre of the room, until stopped off by an apple tree, it was made certain
that this had been occupied by a complete circular medallion, which may,
or may not, have contained a figure, but which was framed similarly by
the above classic borders.' This description, together with a very poor
photograph, indicates that this may have been a large saltire bordered by
swastika pattern and guilloche, with a medallion in the centre, semi-circles
between the arms and a quarter-circle in each corner.
Illustrations Builder CXXII (1922) 872 & JRS XI (1921) pl XX
c. A square mosaic with plain borders has a central guilloche diamond
framing a stylised flower. On the outer sides of this are four (?) ivy leaves
and four guilloche 'L' shapes set in plainly decorated perspective boxes.
There is an almost identical design at Silchester, in Hampshire, Insula
XIV.2.12.
Illustration Builder CXXII (1922) 873
17. Victoria Road (Lock's Timber Yard)   2nd cent   f 1947
In Corinium Museum
Part of a large twelve octagon grid was all that could be excavated on the
site, and this had unfortunately already been much damaged by building
operations. The surviving fragments show six guilloche bordered octagons,
two with a medallion framing a single pelta and the remainder holding stylised
flowers.
Illustration TBGAS LXVII (1946-8) pl III
18. Watermoor Road (Parsonage Field)   f 1958   Fragment in Corinium
Museum
Building 2 (Room 2)
Hasty rescue excavations revealed part of a large house with a long red
tessellated corridor and an interesting geometric mosaic. A large square has
an attractive meander border and, on one side only, a narrow panel of brick
pattern. A central roundel holds a badly damaged urn, flanked by panels
framing shallow fluted drinking cups with two handles. The remainder of
the ground is filled with symmetrically placed panels of all shapes framing
a variety of stylised flowers, foliate scroll, leaves, peltae, duplex knots and
guilloche. The most striking features being a panel with a scroll of trefoils

3A (*right*)
Walton Heath,
Surrey. Geometric
with central urn.
(From coloured
drawing by
J. Baber)

3B (*left*)
Brantingham,
Yorkshire.
Goddesses and
nymphs

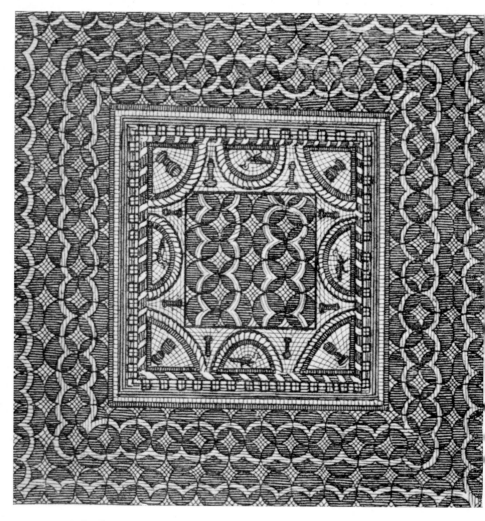

4 Caerleon, Monmouthshire. Geometric with birds and wine-cups. (From engraving in Camden's *Britannia*, 1695, reprinted 1971)

and lotus flower, and another with drooping leaves, each in a separate compartment formed by little columns and arches. In unequal-sided hexagons along the edges of the mosaic one type of segmented flower has two petals made of ivy leaves with arrow-headed stalks, and in another is a unique motif, presumably intended as a lotus bud on a stalk, and somewhat resembling motifs set on the back of peltae at Brislington in Somerset.
Illustration Forthcoming publication of TBGAS
Barton Farm, Cirencester   see **BARTON FARM**

CLANVILLE (Weyhill), Hants
SU 3148   f 1897

A small aisled villa had one good mosaic of which only fragments of guilloche borders remained.
a. (Room 2)
   A floor of plain grey tesserae with three interlaced circles in the same grey, set to one side of the room.
b. (Rooms 4 & 5)
   Two small square floors executed in simple stripes and chequers.
   Reference Arch LVI (1898) 1

COLCHESTER *(Camulodunum)*, Essex
TL 9925

A *colonia* built in a rectangle and covering about 108 acres had a grid of streets laid out to form some 40 *insulae* enclosed by a wall which is now one of the best preserved Roman walls in Britain. A number of temples and houses have been discovered, both within and without the walls, but the mosaics are often fragmentary due to continuous occupation of the town from Roman times until the present day. In addition to the mosaics listed below, plain red tessellated pavements may be seen in Castle Park and in the wall of East Hill House, next to the bus station.
1. Insula 2
a. 45 North Hill   f 1825   Fragment in Colchester & Essex Museum
   Re-excavation in 1906 revealed a border of formal ivy leaf and lotus bud scroll, which encloses an all-over pattern of nine squares and four diamonds framing a variety of stylised flowers, interspersed with panels of guilloche, duplex knots and flowers. This is a more ornate version of a mosaic found at Brislington in Somerset.
   Illustration Hull (1958) pl XV
b. 17/18 North Hill   f 1906   2nd cent   In Colchester & Essex Museum
   In 1925 this mosaic was re-excavated and moved to the Museum. It has a striking geometric pattern of perspective boxes framing panels of peltae

53

and stylised flowers, one of which has been clumsily reset. In the centre a large flower is framed by eight panels of guilloche forming an octagon.
Illustration Hull (1958) pl XVI

2. Insula 9 (Mr Hall's garden, North Hill)   f 1865

a. Fragment reset in Colchester & Essex Museum
About a quarter of this mosaic survived, showing that there must have been four guilloche bordered squares, probably all framing flowers, interspersed with triangles, set round a central diamond.
Illustration TEAS os IV (1869) pl II

b. A fragment, possibly of grid pattern, with a duplex knot in one corner.
Illustration TEAS os IV (1869) pl III

3. Insula 10 (North Hill)

a. f 1922   Large fragment in Colchester & Essex Museum
A fragment of grid pattern in guilloche, with a duplex knot or a stylised flower in each surviving corner panel and a guilloche lozenge or a band of ivy leaf and lotus bud scroll in each rectangular panel.
Illustration TEAS ns XVI (1923) 251

b. f 1965   2nd cent (?)   Fragments stored in Colchester & Essex Museum
A town house with tessellated and mosaic pavements, probably laid in the 2nd century.
i. A clever geometric design composed of perspective boxes, decorated with lozenge swastikas, framing duplex knots and 'L' shaped guilloche bordered panels. The central square holds a large stylised flower with heart-shaped petals and unusual meandering leafy tendrils. Small triangles round the edge contain various arrangements of peltae, some with curious bulbous 'legs'.
Illustration Arch J CXXIII (1966) pl VI
ii. A large square of guilloche grid pattern superimposed on concentric circles of wave crests, ivy leaf scroll and guilloche. The central square has a border of ivy leaf ribbon scroll enclosing a medallion framing a large urn; in each spandrel is a small lotus urn. A large rectangular panel on one side has perspective boxes, decorated with duplex knots and one central ivy leaf, framing medallions with stylised flowers and two small urns.
Illustration Arch J CXXIII (1966) pl VII
iii. Another design with a guilloche grid pattern superimposed on concentric circles of wave crests, ivy leaf scroll, guilloche and an inner ring of bead and reel, a very rare motif in Britain also represented in a crude form in House XII S at Caerwent in Monmouthshire. The central panel holds a 'dahlia', which is almost identical to one found in a similar design at Verulamium in Hertfordshire.
Illustration Arch J CXXIII (1966) pl VIII

4. Insula 11 (North Hill)   f 1938
A small mosaic set on a ground of red tesserae has a Maltese cross in a central medallion within a square, bordered by twists of guilloche, triangles and small concentric circles.
Illustration Photograph and drawing in Colchester & Essex Museum
5. Insula 12 (Bear Lane)   f 1793   Lost (?)
A very fragmentary square mosaic has an inner border of delicate foliate scroll enclosing a large circle with borders of wave crests, triangles and ribbon pattern. In each spandrel is a large fluted urn.
Illustration Vetusta Monumenta III (1796) pl XXXIX
6. Insula 18 (People's Hall, now St George's Hall)   f 1849
    Illustration in Colchester & Essex Museum
A striking floor of black and white chequers with narrow red border and bands of black and white.
Illustration Hull (1958) pl XXIVa
7. Insula 19 (The Cups, High Street)   f 1763   Illustration in Colchester
    & Essex Museum
A small fragment shows a corner, presumably part of the grid design so popular in Colchester, with a stylised flower and lozenges.
Illustration Hull (1958) pl XXIIIa
8. Insula 26 (Culver Street)   exc 1886   Fragments stored in
    Colchester & Essex Museum
A fragment of mosaic with large swastikas forming the border for a pattern of black and white perspective boxes, decorated with a swastika, a plain cross and guilloche 'L' shapes, framing a square with a four-petalled flower.
Illustration TEAS ns III (1889) 207
9. Insula 28 (Red Lion Hotel)
A great number of tessellated and mosaic pavements have been found on or near this site.
a.   f 1857   Illustration in Colchester & Essex Museum
    A fragment from a large pavement shows most of an uneven-sided octagon with borders of lozenges and trefoils, enclosing a medallion edged with guilloche and ribbon pattern and a central stylised flower.
    Illustration Hull (1958) pl XXIVb
b.   f 1882   Fragment in Red Lion Hotel
    A corner with a border of guilloche and three small traingles.
    Illustration Hull (1958) pl XXIVc
10. Insula 34 (near Public Library)   f 1881   Covered over in situ
A small area of perspective box pattern enclosing panels of duplex knots and ivy leaf scroll, frames a large fluted urn. An attractive design, but spoilt by heavy guilloche borders.
Illustration Hull (1958) pl XXXIII

55

11. **Insula 38** (Queen Street) f 1892 Fragments stored in Colchester & Essex Museum (?)
Of a very large mosaic found under 18 Queen Street, a fragment showed eight-pointed stars and guilloche.
Reference Hull (1958) 212

12. **Insula 40** (Beryfield) f 1923 In Colchester & Essex Museum
A simple grid pattern mosaic has a stylised flower with heart-shaped petals in a central medallion and a smaller version in each corner square. In each rectangle is a crudely executed but amusing sea-beast pursuing a dolphin, a theme more skilfully employed in Dyer Street, Cirencester in Gloucestershire.
Illustration Hull (1958) pl XXXIV

13. **Victoria Inn** (outside town walls) f 1880
A fragment is reconstructed in a drawing to show four panels of black swastika pattern on a white ground, each enclosing a strip of coloured guilloche. Of five square panels only that in the centre survived to show a coloured duplex knot (?) bordered by guilloche.
Illustration TEAS ns II (1884) 189

COLERNE, Wilts
ST 8171

Some eleven rooms of a villa were uncovered, one mosaic having been found in 1838 and reburied without any record being made, and when reopened during the excavations of 1854 only fragments of the borders remained.

a. (Room 1) f 1838 Lost
'From the descriptions of those persons in the neighbourhood who visited the pavement in 1838, it appears that the design consisted of a chariot, with a charioteer and four horses abreast. Some persons in the parish remembered seeing an inscription or word above the chariot, which the parish clerk told me was either SERVIUS or SEVERUS, but this I found no one could confirm . . . ' The 1854 excavator, E W Godwin, wrote that it had a border of guilloche and that in two of the corners 'fragments of a kind of wheel pattern . . . could, after some difficulty, be traced.'
Reference Arch J XIII (1856) 328

b. (Room 2) f 1854
A square, with plain blue swastikas enclosing five small panels framing duplex knots and hourglass triangles, is flanked by two panels of guilloche, the whole being bordered by badly executed swastikas, which in one place deteriorate into a simple meander!
Illustration Soc of Ant of London Top Colls (Brown Port Wilts)

c. f 1854
An outer border of large chequers lies round a square of shaded interlaced circles bordered by swastikas enclosing hourglass triangles. On one side

adjacent panels of guilloche, lozenges, stepped triangles, shaded interlaced circles and chequers could be part of the floor of a corridor.
Illustration Soc of Ant of London Top Colls (Brown Port Wilts)

COLESBOURNE, Glos   see COMB END

COLLINGHAM (Dalton Parlours), Yorks
SE 4044   f 1854   Apse in Yorkshire Museum, York

Part of a large villa with hypocausts and bath was excavated in 1854, when one apsed room with an ill-assorted mosaic was discovered. According to a small drawing, the main part of the floor has a grid of squares along one side of the room and the remainder covered with shaded scale pattern cut transversely by a scroll of ivy leaves flowing round a fluted urn filled with fruit. In the centre a distraught-looking head of Medusa, with an 'M' of ribbon dangling beneath her chin, is placed looking away from the main body of the room. The head is flanked by two strands of guilloche and two lotus urns.
Illustrations Yorks Phil Soc Proc I (1849-54) pl 7 & Yorkshire Museum postcard.

COMB END (Colesbourne), Glos
SO 9811   Lost

Extensive ruins of a villa were accidentally unearthed in 1779 and 1787 and further excavated by Lysons in 1794.
a. (Corridor 1)   f 1779
   A long corridor with alternate panels of concentric diamonds and chequers, interspersed with concentric squares, small chequers and duplex knots.
   Illustrations Arch IX (1789) pl XX fig 1 & Soc of Ant of London Top Colls (Red Port Glos) 17
b. f 1787
   A mosaic was said to have shown 'many figures of birds and fishes.'
   Reference Arch IX (1789) 319
c. (Room 4)   f 1794
   A border of swastika pattern apparently encloses panels of shaded interlaced circles, diamonds and unusual two-coloured 'C' shapes set back to back in pairs.
   Illustration Lysons II (1817) pl II
d. (Corridor 7)   f 1794
   Another corridor with blue and white chequers and several stripes of brown.
   Reference Arch XVIII (1817) 112

COMBE ST NICHOLAS (Wadeford), Somerset
ST 3010   4th cent (?)   Lost
A number of mosaic pavements were found in what must have been a large villa.
a. f 1810
Ten octagons formed by the arms of swastikas hold two varieties of stylised flowers. Large peltae fill the spaces round the edges and there is one narrow border panel of diamonds.
Illustration PSANHS I (1849-50) pl I
b. f 1810
A square bordered by swastika pattern, holds a guilloche bordered octagon framing two interlaced guilloche squares with a central rainbow-shaded medallion. Each corner has a heavy foliate spray.
Illustration Drawing in Somerset County Museum, Taunton
c. f 1861
A striking labyrinth pattern in red on white.
Illustration PSANHS XIII (1865-6) pl 3
d. A corridor of chequer pattern.
Illustration PSANHS XIII (1865-6) pl 6
e. A haphazard arrangement of 'T' shapes, 'L' shapes and squares executed in coarse tesserae.
Illustration PSANHS XIII (1865-6) pl 18
f. Various borders from fine mosaic floors include a good piece of awning pattern.
Illustration PSANHS XIII (1865-6) pl 12

COMBLEY, IOW
SZ 5387   3rd cent (?)   f circa 1867   In situ
A small, but fairly luxurious villa with mosaic and tessellated pavements.
a. (Room 3)
A long rectangular mosaic with two surviving squares, one containing a large octagon, with a duplex knot in the central medallion surrounded by four shaded peltae with shaded semi-circles between their 'feet'. Two spandrels hold lotus urns and two hold peltae urns, all with leafy tendril handles. The adjacent square, much damaged, has two plain interlaced squares framing a large medallion with a chequered border and a central stylised flower with four ivy leaf petals.
b. (Room 5)
A narrow room leading to a semi-circular bath has a fragmentary panel of swastika pattern with alternate strands of red and blue enclosing two attractive dolphins, probably executed in much the same style as those at Bramdean in Hampshire. This type of two-coloured swastika pattern may

also be found at Latimer in Buckinghamshire and Withington in Gloucestershire.
Reference Isle of Wight Natural History & Archaeological Society Proceedings VI (1970)

COTTERSTOCK, Northants
TL 0390

a. f 1736
An attractive pavement with a broad border of swastika pattern and panels of guilloche enclosing a square of perspective boxes. Four 'L' shapes of meander and guilloche frame a central diamond holding a flower with four heart-shaped petals.
Illustration Artis (1828) pl LX
b. f 1798
Within a square border of 'Z' pattern, a large urn of unusual shape is decorated with a heart and has a streamer with ivy leaves draped over the top. There are rectangular panels of peltae pattern on two sides.
Illustrations Artis (1828) pl LIX & VCH Northamptonshire I (1902) fig 21

CRONDALL, Hants
SU 7947   f 1817   Lost   Sampler in Crondall Parish Church

The only mosaic known to have been found here has a grid of nine guilloche bordered octagons, each holding a medallion framing alternately a flower and a lotus urn, and in the centre an urn in a wreath.
Illustration Country Life 25 June 1969

DALTON PARLOURS   see COLLINGHAM

DAVENTRY (Borough Hill), Northants
SP 5863   f 1823

A number of tessellated and mosaic pavements were found here.
a. (Room J)
'Fragments of two sides of a tessellated pavement was found, composed of blue, yellow, red and white tesserae, half an inch square, forming an outer border of the foliated Vitruvian scroll, and an inner one of the simple guilloche, within which was a small ornamented circle, evidently the commencement of a central pattern.'
Reference Morgan (1886) 122
b. (Room K)   Fragment in Central Museum, Northampton
Within borders of stepped triangles and guilloche, two interlaced guilloche squares frame a medallion, with contents destroyed. Lotus buds occupy

DAVENTRY

each of the four outer spandrels.
Illustration Smith, C R (1848) pl XLII

DENTON, Lincs
SK 8730   4th cent   f 1727

First found in 1727, much of this villa was uncovered again in 1949 before its final destruction by opencast mining. It was found to have at least seven rooms with simple tessellated floors.
a. (Room 2)
An all-over pattern of heavy interlaced octagons forming decorated lozenges and squares.
Illustration Fowler (1796-1818) 10
b. (Room 7)
A square mosaic with perspective boxes, decorated with stippling and duplex knots, forming a central eight-pointed star.
Illustration Smith, D J (1969) pl 3.26
c. (Room 9)
A long room or corridor with a panel of simple grid pattern.
Illustration LAAS X ns (1964) pl 7

DEWLISH, Dorset
SY 7797   4th cent   f 1740   Covered over in situ

A corridor villa was first found when a tree blew down in 1740 revealing a mosaic composed of coarse black and white tesserae, and re-excavations, which began in 1969, have uncovered several simple mosaic pavements.
a. f 1969
An exploratory trench revealed a small area of corridor with a Greek key pattern executed in black and red on a white ground.
b. (Room 1)   f 1971
An effective pattern of very small red and white chequers.
c. (Room 3)   f 1971
A narrow panel executed in fine tesserae, set in a coarse grey tessellated ground, has a line of touching circles, each containing the cushion-shape usually formed by the interlacing of circles.
d. (Room 4)   f 1971
A room with a hypocaust has a rectangular apse with large red and white chequers. Small fragments of a finer mosaic in the main part of the room indicate borders of guilloche and wave crests.
e. (Room 6)   f 1971
A panel of Greek key pattern, similar to a. above, but in black on a white ground, runs the length of the corridor so far uncovered. Although this

60

design is unique for corridors in Britain, Frampton has passages with very similar meander and swastika patterns.

f. (Room 7)   f 1971
A coarse tessellated pavement with one white stripe down the centre.

g. (Room 8)   f 1971
Coarse red and grey stripes

h. (Room 9)   f 1971
Fragments surviving over a hypocaust showed lines of bisected chequers in red and white, executed in fine tesserae, and reminiscent of the borders to the two urns at Olga Road in Dorchester.
Illustrations Photographs in Dorset County Museum, Dorchester & PDNHAS 93 (1972) figs 17-21

DORCHESTER *(Durnovaria)*, Dorset
SY 6990

A *civitas* capital of some 80 acres, with the lines of the Roman fortifications preserved by tree-lined walks. No public buildings or baths have so far been discovered. A remarkable open aqueduct brought water to the town from a point in the River Frome a little upstream from the building at Frampton. References to the following mosaics may be found in RCHM Dorset II.3 (1970) 553-70.

1. Colliton Park   Building I   4th cent   f 1937
An 'L' shaped house in the north-west corner of the town had eight rooms with mosaic floors which, with the exception of Room 8, have all been covered over in situ.
Illustration RCHM Dorset II.3 (1970) facing 557 (plan)

a. (Room 8)   On view in situ
Stepped triangles and four swastikas enclosing chequers surround a rectangular panel with a colourful design in finer tesserae. A large saltire, heavily bordered with guilloche and decorated with duplex knots, has a central guilloche bordered medallion framing a four-petalled stylised flower against a shaded background.
Illustration RCHM Dorset II.3 (1970) pl 220

b. (Room 10)
A border of swastikas, chequers and one panel of guilloche, set under a window, surrounds a grid of sixteen (?) guilloche bordered octagons, within each of which is a medallion with borders of 'Z' pattern or guilloche enclosing a stylised flower.
Illustration RCHM Dorset II.3 (1970) pl 220

c. (Room 13)
A long narrow corridor room has a coarse red and white mosaic with a

61

border of chequers surrounding an all-over pattern of swastikas enclosing small concentric squares.
Illustration RCHM Dorset II.3 (1970) pl 219

d. (Room 14)

Coarse tesserae arranged in broad red and grey stripes.
Illustration RCHM Dorset II.3 (1970) facing 557 (plan)

e. (Room 15)

A large room with a very fine mosaic, of which only fragments remained, has a wide border of swastikas enclosing panels of guilloche and chequers. Of the design in the main area of the room there survived only two rainbow bordered medallions framing female heads, one hooded and the other with ringlets and flowers, probably representing two of the Seasons.
Illustration RCHM Dorset II.3 (1970) facing 557 (plan) & pl 218

f. (Room 16)

In another narrow corridor room only a small fragment survived, which may have shown a diagonal grid in white on a red ground.
Illustration RCHM Dorset II.3 (1970) facing 557 (plan)

g. (Room 17)

Small fragments of a border of swastikas enclosing rectangles and two medallions.
Illustration RCHM Dorset II.3 (1970) pl 219

h. (Room 18)

Fragments of coarse tessellated borders in white meander pattern, stepped triangles, swastikas and concentric rectangles.
Illustration RCHM Dorset II.3 (1970) pl 219

2. Building VI   4th cent (?)   f 1938

a. (North Room)   Lost

A square, flanked by two guilloche panels, holds a large saltire, of which only part of the outline survived. One semi-circle between the arms of the cross frames a form of lotus flower hitherto unknown in Britain and one of the corners has a conventional lotus bud with a wedge-shaped stalk.
Illustration RCHM Dorset II.3 (1970) pl 224

b. (South Room)

A narrow rectangular room with borders of triangles and guilloche, has a strip of shaded interlaced octagons framing duplex knots and triangles.
Illustration RCHM Dorset II.3 (1970) pl 222

3. Durngate Street   4th cent (?)   f 1905   In Dorset County Museum, Dorchester   plate 11

A mosaic was found whilst digging the foundations for a school attached to the Primitive Methodist Chapel, now the Salvation Army Hall. A large guilloche bordered circle within a square encloses interlaced guilloche squares round a medallion with borders of guilloche and 'Z' pattern. In the centre is a

62

four-petalled stylised flower, the petals interspersed with four acanthus leaves forming a cross. There is a large urn in each spandrel; out of two rise crested snakes, the third has an arrangement of leaf sprays and the fourth has two leaves issuing from the foot. Flanking the square are two wide panels of swastika pattern, one enclosing guilloche and two duplex knots. The two snakes should be compared with the tail of the Chimaera at Hinton St Mary.
Illustration RCHM Dorset II.3 (1970) pl 223 (202)

4. Fordington High Street (Lott & Walne)   4th cent (?)   f 1903
    In Dorset County Museum, Dorchester
Not more than fifty yards outside the town walls, on the road leading to the east, is a building presumed to be a town house. The plain tessellated border in fine tesserae was found in 1903 and thought to be a corridor, but re-excavation in 1927 revealed a brightly coloured mosaic executed in small tesserae. The dominating feature is a horseshoe apse with heavy guilloche borders framing a rather sinister-looking head or mask of Neptune, scarlet seaweed sprouting from his head and beard, flanked by dolphins and fishes. A floral and foliate scroll, springing from the base of a central urn, leads to the main area of the room, ehich is divided by guilloche into nine octagons, each holding a medallion framing a stylised flower. Two medallions have rainbow-shaded (?) borders bound with ribbon, very similar to the border of a panel in a mosaic from Dyer Street in Cirencester. The central octagon is lost, but as there was no medallion it may well have framed a figure or figured scene; there is one narrow border with an indifferent foliate scroll.
Illustration RCHM Dorset II.3 (1970) Frontispiece

5. 23 Glyde Path Road
a. f circa 1810
    A corridor with longitudinal red and grey bands in coarse tesserae was first discovered when an apple tree was planted in the garden, but it was not fully cleared until 1880
    Illustration Plan in Dorset County Museum, Dorchester
b. f 1966
    One foot square red and grey chequers in coarse tesserae.
    Illustration Photograph in Dorset County Museum, Dorchester

6. 37 Glyde Path Road   f 1957
A small fragment of mosaic in six colours may have shown part of a grid of circles and octagons. The medallion has an unusual border of Greek key pattern enclosing an ivy leaf, and the octagon frames a medallion bordered with guilloche.
Illustration PDNHAS 81 (1959) pl Ib

7. Icen Way (All Saints Glebe)
A number of discoveries of mosaics and loose tesserae at the junction of Icen Way and All Saints Road, as well as under the adjacent Gas Works, may

63

indicate the presence of one large town house.

a. Lost

An almost perfect square mosaic in small red, white and black tesserae was seen in use as the kitchen floor of a cottage in the year 1850.

Reference RCHM Dorset II.3 (1970) 567

b. f 1897   Fragment in All Saints Rectory

A corridor of grey tesserae leads from a coarse mosaic floor of red and grey chequers, much of which was relaid in the High School in Dorchester, Massachusetts in the United States of America

Illustration Plan in Dorset County Museum, Dorchester

8. The Prison

A number of mosaic pavements have been found within the confines of the prison walls, the site of a Norman castle and of three successive prison buildings.

a. f circa 1809

A corridor, with concentric blue rectangles set singly and in pairs on a white ground, was found to the west of the prison and adjacent to a mosaic discovered at 23 Glyde Path Road.

Illustration Soc of Ant of London Top Colls (Red Port Dorset)

b. f 1841

A pattern of lozenges executed in large tesserae was found in the prison burial ground.

Reference Dorset County Chronicle 7 January 1841

c. f 1854   Fragments in Dorset County Museum, Dorchester

Fragments of guilloche border

d. f 1858   In Dorset County Museum, Dorchester

Governor J V D Lawrance excavated part of a range of rooms with mosaics, one in perfect condition and two from which only guilloche bordered medallions and a circle survived. The former is a large mosaic with numerous broad bands of coarse red, white and grey tesserae round a square with borders of 'Z' pattern and small diagonal chequers in four colours; these in turn enclose two plain interlaced squares forming a shaded octagon and framing a central medallion with two hearts, one on a grey and the other on a red ground.

Illustrations RCHM Dorset II.3 (1970) pl 224 & photograph and drawing in Dorset County Museum, Dorchester

9. Somerleigh Court

Over the years a number of mosaic and tessellated floors have been found in the grounds of a private house, now an extension of the Dorset County Hospital.

a. f 1862   Covered over in situ

The construction of Somerleigh Court led to the discovery of a fragment

of what was thought to be a plain white pavement, with one border of decorated interlaced circles round heart-shaped devices, divided by a narrow band of triangles from another border with shaded peltae; the whole being executed in seven colours.
Illustration Moule, H J Dorchester Antiquities (1906) fig 1 & coloured drawing in Dorset County Museum, Dorchester

b. f 1889
A large fragment of mosaic described in a local newspaper as having 'a beautiful rose pattern, the "rose" being nearly 2 ft. in diameter, and almost perfect in all its details.' It was said to have been executed in small cream, black, red, buff and turquoise tesserae.
Reference Dorset County Chronicle 1 August 1889

c. f 1889   Fragment in porch of Somerleigh Court
Blocks of four plain black swastikas alternate with two foot square panels framing a guilloche mat and a guilloche bordered medallion. The general design appears to be very similar to that of the mosaic found in Mr Templeman's garden in South Street.
Illustration Photograph in Dorset County Museum, Dorchester

d. f 1963
A coarse mosaic of red and grey chequers, excavated in 1963, is probably the same as one found in 1875
Illustration Photograph in Dorset County Museum, Dorchester

10.   45 South Street   f 1905   Lost
Found at the back of these premises, close to Trinity Street, a fragmentary geometric mosaic has two interlaced guilloche squares enclosing a central medallion, with contents destroyed.
Illustration Photograph in Dorset County Museum, Dorchester

11. 48 South Street
Several as yet unrelated mosaic floors have been found in this area.

a. (Cedar Park)   f 1894   In Dorset County Museum, Dorchester
A simple grid in red on a grey ground, unusual only in that the lines running one way are broader than the others; there is a small white rectangle at each intersection.
Illustration Photograph in Dorset County Museum, Dorchester

b. (Marks & Spencer)   f 1936
A fragment of red swastika pattern border.
Illustration Drawing in Dorset County Museum, Dorchester

c. (Marks & Spencer)   f 1935 (?)
A fragment of concentric red rectangles.
Illustration Drawing in Dorset County Museum, Dorchester

12.   49 (?) South Street (Mr Templeman's garden)   f circa 1725
A large piece of mosaic with blocks of four plain swastikas alternating with

at least six square panels framing stylised flowers, and one border of lozenges. *Illustration Hutchins II (1863) facing 692*

13.   50 South Street (Devon & Cornwall Bank)   f 1899   Fragment in Dorset County Museum, Dorchester

Fragments of a fine mosaic apparently show a border of guilloche panels and a corner square framing a stylised flower. A contemporary volume of *The Builder* states that 'It is a very simple affair, divided into spaces by parallel bands with an ordinary form of guilloche ornament between them; an octagon centre panel with a circular centre.

Illustration Photograph in Dorset County Museum, Dorchester & Reference Builder LXXVII (1899) 602

14.   26 Trinity Street (Tilley's Showrooms)

Several fragments found on this site, which is adjacent to Somerleigh Court, may all come from the same building.

a. f 1925

Three fragments, perhaps belonging to the same pavement, were found and described in a local newspaper.

i. 'A panel has a red and white design down the centre on a black background with a bordering in white and black.'

ii. A fragment now under a concrete floor was 'in black and white mosaic squares, with a centre-piece of red and white squares.'

iii. 'An elongated triangle in black and white.' A tracing by O C Vidler made in 1925 shows borders of guilloche and right-angled black and white triangles, and one lozenge, but it is not known whether it relates to the fragment just described.

Illustration Drawing in Dorset County Museum, Dorchester Reference Dorset County Chronicle 25 June 1925

b. f 1967   One panel on view in situ

A corridor found near the previous mosaics and running towards Somerleigh Court, was divided into a series of square panels enclosing plain concentric circles and a guilloche bordered medallion.

Illustration Photograph in Dorset County Museum, Dorchester Reference RCHM Dorset II.3 (1970) 563

15.   South West Corner   f 1841   Lost

The exact location of this fragmentary mosaic is not known, but since it was said to have been found in a field belonging to Mr Barnes, a builder, it could have been on the site of the Southern Electricity Board buildings in Trinity Street or under Whetstone's Almshouses on West Walks. 'The whole of the floor of the *coenaculum* (dining room) has been destroyed at some early period, leaving only a portion of guilloche border, with an outer border of spiral and circular ornaments. From this the floor of the *zotheca* (alcove), which was formed of a very favourite pattern in such pavements, was divided

by a series of large lozenges.'
Reference Gents Mag (1841) 413

16. Olga Road   SY 6890   f 1899   In Dorset County Museum, Dorchester
plate 6

In the course of building the Victoria Park Estate, outside the Roman town walls, five mosaics from three contiguous rooms, probably belonging to a villa rather than to a town house, were found.

i. A very fragmentary small rectangle with a border of stepped triangles and a central guilloche bordered medallion.

ii. A small rectangular 'mat' bordered with guilloche has a large fluted urn in a circle, flanked by white triangles on a black ground.

iii. A large rectangle bordered by swastikas enclosing panels of guilloche and lozenges with geometric devices. A central square has in each corner a pelta with the outer points terminating in spirals and leaves and the central point in a convoluted ivy leaf; it encloses a large guilloche bordered octagon framing a sixteen-petalled flower with a central duplex knot. The square is flanked by four small squares, each pair linked by a narrow panel with a unique spray of leaves, and containing guilloche mats or a stylised flower within a guilloche border.

iv. A 'mat' similar to ii above, but the urn, set in a rectangle, is taller and the flanking triangles are black on a white ground.

v. A guilloche rectangle has two saltires, the central medallions framing stylised flowers with lotus bud and ivy leaf petals and the arms of the crosses decorated with pairs of leaves and geometric devices. This mosaic has several features in common with one floor at Halstock.
Illustration PDNHAS XXI (1900) facing 162

DOWNTON, Wilts
SU 1821   4th cent   f 1753   In Salisbury & South Wiltshire Museum
plate 9A

A simple corridor villa with several tessellated and at least two mosaic floors, of which only one survived.

a. (Room 1)
A square mosaic has a large guilloche bordered octagon, within which two interlaced guilloche squares frame a medallion with a wave crest border. In the centre is an attractive fluted urn with dolphin handles and in the outer corners are ivy leaves with tendrils and foliate sprays.
Illustration WAM LVIII (1963) pl I

DROITWICH *(Salinae)*, **Worcs**
SO 8963   f 1847   Restored fragment in City Museum, Worcester

DROITWICH

In this small walled town two badly damaged mosaics were found, one with a duplex knot in a guilloche bordered medallion.
Illustration VCH Worcestershire I (1901) 210

EAST COKER, Somerset
ST 5413   4th cent (?)

The mosaics found in this villa were of exceptional interest, but unfortunately only a line drawing of one and a fragment of another remain.
a. f 1753   Lost
> A contemporary account in the *Gentleman's Magazine* refers to a mosaic executed in strong colours, 'representing a woman lying in full proportion, with an hour glass under her elbow, and a flower pot in one hand . . . Within a beautiful square, containing a circle, are these figures: A woman drest, 'tis thought, in the Roman stola with its purple laticlave, or border; another much damaged; which with the former, each give a hand to fix the cloths round another woman, laid on a couch naked down to below her waist, and on whom the physician hard by prepares to do some operation by the fire, either cupping or burning able to suit the use of the room.'
> This interesting scene, set in a large circle within a rectangle, must certainly be interpreted in its mythological rather than its medical context! The meaning is nevertheless somewhat obscure, but it could depict the miraculous birth of Bacchus, with Semele lying naked on the couch awaiting the appearance of Zeus from the thundercloud which looms overhead. Hera (?) wearing a regal crown and an old man holding aloft either a cornucopia or the torch of life, in expectation of the birth of Bacchus, are both directing attention to Semele. Ino, the sister of Semele, may have been the woman said to have been standing behind the couch giving 'a hand to fix the cloths', but since the description and the illustration of the mosaic do not tally in every detail, it is by no means certain that there was another person, nor is it known which version is the more correct. The spandrels hold busts of the Seasons or of the Wind gods in the guise of Mercury, and above the medallion a dog with a curly tail is chasing a hare and below another is hunting a stag.
> *Illustration Smith, D J (1969) fig 3.3   Reference Gents Mag (1753) 293*
b. f 1753   Lost
> A purely geometric design which includes lozenges, octagons and peltae.
> *Reference VCH Somerset I (1906) 329*
c. f 1818   Fragment stored in Somerset County Museum, Taunton
> A fragment shows two huntsmen carrying between them a deer, tied by the feet to a pole, while a dog sits looking eagerly up at the kill. There is an extraordinary similarity in clothing, hairstyle and general composition between this and similar scenes found in the Mediterranean area.

5 Micklegate Bar, York. Deer and venison. (From engraving by W. Fowler; photograph RCHM)

Illustration VCH Somerset I (1906) fig 87

EAST CREECH (Furzebrook, Church Knowle), Dorset
SY 9382   f 1888

A villa, situated near the ancient shale route from Kimmeridge to Wareham, has produced one coarse mosaic pavement. A simple grid of squares has a small square in the centre of each panel and is executed in red on a white ground.
Illustration Photograph in Dorset County Museum, Dorchester   Reference RCHM Dorset II.3 (1970) 595

EAST MALLING, Kent
TQ 7057   f 1955

The section of a villa, excavated in 1955 and 1965, revealed a small fragment of wall mosaic showing one pelta, thought to be part of a frieze of peltae.
Illustration Arch Cant LXXI (1957) facing 228

EBRINGTON, Glos
SP 1939   2nd cent (?)   f 1956

Excavations revealed a corridor and two large rooms with simple tessellated pavements and a big hall with a plain black grid of squares, a small cross in the centre of each square.
Illustration Photograph in records of RCHM

ECCLES, Kent
TQ 7260   1st cent   f 1965

A very large building, which remained in occupation throughout the years of Roman rule in Britain, has a number of tessellated floors and some of the earliest mosaics to be found in the country.
a. (Room 30)
    Very small fragments of mosaic, found in the *frigidarium*, have been imaginatively reconstructed in a drawing to show two gladiators fighting within a central guilloche bordered square, which is set in perspective boxes decorated with four-petalled flowers and single ivy leaves.
    Illustrations Arch Cant LXXX (1965) frontispiece and fig 2
b. (Room 31)
    A few fragments of fine tesserae, found in the plunge bath, show a dolphin.
    Illustration Arch Cant LXXX (1965) fig 4

EXETER *(Isca Dumnoniorum)*, **Devon**
SX 9192

A *civitas* capital of 92 acres lying on the estuary of the River Exe, has produced numerous tessellated pavements and a few fragmentary mosaics. One of simple geometric pattern, found in Pancras Lane in 1837, was relaid in the old City Police Station, now demolished.
St Catherine's Almshouses   3rd cent   f 1945
Two rooms with panels of duplex knots and guilloche.
Illustration Fox, A. Roman Exeter (Manchester 1952) pl VII

EXNING see LANDWADE

FIFEHEAD NEVILLE, Dorset
ST 7711   4th cent   f 1880

The discovery of an unusual mosaic pavement in 1880 led to the excavations in 1902, which revealed one wing of a large villa with several mosaic floors.
a. (Floor 1)   f 1880   Coloured drawing in Dorset County Museum, Dorchester
   A square has a large central fluted urn surrounded by two concentric circular friezes of fishes and dolphins, with stylised floral and foliate sprays in the spandrels. On two sides are bands of shaded meander pattern and the whole is bordered by large 'T' shapes.
   Illustrations Smith, D J (1969) pl 3.30 & photograph in Dorset County Museum, Dorchester
b. (Floor 2)   f 1903   Coloured drawing (without bust) in Dorset County Museum, Dorchester
   There are two contemporary drawings of a mosaic with a large saltire and a flowing border of foliate scroll. The central medallion has two borders of shaded 'revolving' leaves, and in one version they frame the helmeted head of a female (?) with a staff over the shoulder. A duplex knot in a plain medallion decorates each arm of the cross and in each corner is a stylised spray of leaves. In the semi-circles between the arms, one version has four stylised leaf and flower sprays, while the other has only two stylised leaves and two sprays of ivy leaves.
   Illustration RCHM Dorset III.1 (1970) pl 133 (with bust)
c. (Floor 3)
   A badly damaged floor is recorded only by a brief note in a manuscript, 'hypocaust with tessellated floor with heads within a circle.'
   References Oliver, Vere L. ms 'Roman tessellated pavements in Dorset' in Dorset County Museum, Dorchester & RCHM Dorset III.1 (1970) 94

d. (Floor 4)   f 1903
Only a fragment of an unusual border survived, showing a medallion or
part of a scroll framing a cross of leaf sprays interspersed with convoluted
hearts, bisected peltae and more leaf sprays.
Illustration Tracing and photograph in Dorset County Museum, Dorchester
Reference RCHM Dorset III.1 (1970) 94

FISHBOURNE, Sussex
SU 8404

Building at Fishbourne, near Chichester, began soon after the Roman invasion
of England in AD 47, but the earliest structures had no mosaic floors. In AD
75 a very large building was constructed round a formal garden. It has been
suggested that this was the palace of the British King Cogidubnus and his descendants, for he and his tribe had been consistently friendly towards the
Romans from the time of their first landing, but there is little concrete evidence to support this theory. Most of the mosaics were laid during this early
period, but the building was altered extensively in the 2nd century and again
in the early 3rd century, when more mosaics were laid. The 'palace' was
occupied until its destruction by fire at the end of the 3rd century, although
by then it was probably divided into separate dwellings. The numbering of
the rooms has been entirely altered since the completion of excavations and
now runs numerically after the letters W, for west wing, and N for north
wing, and here the old room numbers follow in brackets. A distinctive
feature in most of these mosaics is the plain black and white bands which
form the borders.
a. N 1 (Room 55)   1st cent
   A small fragment of the original floor, beneath a later hypocaust, has been
   reconstructed to show a plain grid of nine squares containing a variety of
   simple geometric forms in colour, with a border of black and white bands.
   Illustration Cunliffe (1971) pls LVIa and LXXXVIa
b. N 2 (Room 54)   2nd cent
   Fragments of a square mosaic with black chequers on one side and on the
   other, black tesserae forming a scatter of tiny crosses on a white ground.
   Illustration Cunliffe (1971) pls LVIa and LXXXVIa
c. N 3 (Room 59)   1st cent
   An attractive design of perspective boxes in simple outline, framing
   various arrangements of squares, all in black on white.
   Illustration Ant J XLIV (1964) pl IIb & Cunliffe (1971) pls XXb and
   LXXVIIa
d. N 4 (Room 60)   1st cent
   A simple grid in white on a black ground with small black squares at the
   intersections.

Illustrations Ant J XLIV (1964) pl IVa & Cunliffe (1971) pls XXI and LXXVIIb

e. N5 (Room 56)   2nd cent

Two large scallop shells form the curved ends of a rectangular panel and between them is a narrow strip with lozenges and two pairs of dolphins in simple outline.

Illustrations Ant J XLIV (1964) pl VIb & Cunliffe (1971) pls LXXXVb and LXXXIXb

f. N 7 (Room 3)   2nd cent

Set in a broad border of black and white chequers, a very well preserved and attractive coloured mosaic has a large guilloche bordered saltire, within a square, the central roundel framing a winged cupid riding on a spirited dolphin. Tall, rather shaky, black urns with tendrils decorate the arms of the cross, and in each semi-circle between them is a lively sea-beast. Quarter-circles in the corners hold shaded scallop shells, which are more delicate and pleasing than the great shell at Verulamium. An attractive scroll of ivy leaves and lotus buds springs from four urns and a minute duck-like bird sits on one of the tendrils.

Illustrations Ant J XLIV (1964) pl V & Cunliffe (1971) pls XLVII-LIII, LXXXIII and LXXXVIII

g. N 8 (Room 5)   3rd cent

A poorly executed mosaic 'mat' has a central duplex knot backed by four semi-circles, framed in a heavy guilloche bordered medallion. Round this are four small urns flanked by dolphins, and a scallop shell occupies each corner. There are two borders of concentric lozenges.

Illustration Cunliffe (1971) pls LVIIIb, LXXXVa and LXXXIXa

h. N 11 (Room 8)   2nd or 3rd cent

A funny little coloured mosaic has a six-petalled flower as the central feature in an apparently haphazard arrangement of black lines, which is either a misguided swastika pattern or an erratic brick pattern. It is impossible to tell what pattern was intended for the border, but it has turned out as an unusual arrangement of ovals and semi-circles in four colours.

Illustrations Ant J XLV (1965) pl VIIIb & Cunliffe (1971) pls LVIc, LXXXVb and XCa

i. N 12 (Room 11)   1st cent

To me this is far and away the most beautiful mosaic at Fishbourne. Unfortunately no photograph can do it justice, as its beauty lies not only in the purity of the geometric design, but also in the colour and smooth texture of the tesserae. The pattern, in black and white, is of simple perspective boxes framing crosses, some decorated with triangles and others with delicate flowers. Two borders are of brick pattern.

Illustrations Ant J XLIV (1964) pl IIIa & Cunliffe (1971) pls XXIV and LXXVIII

j. N 13 (Room 10)

i. 1st cent

A small patch of swastikas enclosing a panel with small squares and rectangles, all in black and white, lies under a later pavement

Illustrations Ant J XLII (1962) pl IXa & Cunliffe (1971) pls XXIIIb and LXXXc

ii. 2nd cent

A very badly executed mosaic has, within a square, a central medallion framing a head of Medusa and a curious pelta urn in each spandrel. Surrounding this are four square panels of black and white chequers and eight octagons with coloured flowers, leaves and duplex knots. There is an assortment of borders of interlaced circles, crude ivy leaf scroll, cushion-shapes, squares and triangles.

Illustrations Ant J XLII (1962) pl XIIa & Cunliffe (1971) pls XLIII and LXXXIV

k. N 14 (Corridor 9)   2nd cent

A fragment of perspective box pattern framing crosses decorated with triangles or little circles, one holding a tiny Maltese cross, surrounded by a brick pattern border, all in black on white. Although perhaps copied from N 12, this rendering was not nearly as successful.

Illustrations Ant J XLV (1965) pl VIIa & Cunliffe (1971) pls XXVa and and LXXXVIa

l. N 19 (Room 18)   1st cent

A square of black and white brick pattern in simple outline.

Illustrations Ant J XLV (1965) pl VIb & Cunliffe (1971) pls XXVa and LXXXd

m. N 20 (Room 19)   1st cent

An attractive square mosaic executed in delicate colours, but unfortunately much damaged, holds a large medallion with borders of guilloche and an unusual wreath of alternate flowers and ivy leaves. In each of two adjacent spandrels is a long necked urn with tendrils, flanked by dolphins, and in the other two are similar urns, but with square handles and leafy scrolls.

Illustrations Ant J XLII (1962) pl XIb & Cunliffe (1971) pls XXVI,XXVII, LXXXI and XCI

n. N 21 (Room 20)   1st cent

A long narrow mosaic with a trellis of plain white interlaced squares on a black ground and alternate red and grey squares along the centre.

Illustrations Ant J XLII (1962) pl XIIb & Cunliffe (1971) pls XXVb and LXXXII

75

o. West Corridor (Room 62)   2nd cent
A very roughly executed pattern of 'T' shapes and chequers in red and grey arranged in squares, similar to the panel in W 6 below.
Illustration Cunliffe (1971) pl LXXXVII
West Wing. Almost half these rooms lie under houses and gardens, making excavation impossible, and the remainder have been covered over in situ.

p. W 3 (Room 67)   1st cent
Bold black swastikas frame panels with a variety of geometric patterns in simple outline, including squares of a small finely drawn swastika pattern.
Illustrations Ant J XLIV (1964) pl IIa & Cunliffe (1971) pls XIIIa and LXXV

q. W 5 (Room 69)   1st cent
A small fragment of simple leaf and tendril scroll.
Illustrations Ant J XLIV (1964) pl IIIb & Cunliffe (1971) pls XIIIb and LXXIV

r. W 6 (Room 70)   1st cent
A fragment shows a corner of the main pattern and a panel of black and white chequers and 'T' shapes arranged in squares.
Illustrations Ant J XLIV (1964) pl IVb & Cunliffe (1971) pls XVIb and LXXIV

s. W 8 (Room 86)   1st cent
An all-over pattern of perspective boxes framing square geometric panels in black and white, with two borders of delicate and colourful foliate scroll, probably springing from central urns.
Illustrations Ant J XLV (1965) pl Vb & Cunliffe (1971) pls XIV and LXXVI

t. W 13 (Room 75)   1st cent
A corridor of white tesserae with borders of two concentric black bands.
Illustrations Cunliffe (1971) pls XVIIa and LXXIV

FOLKESTONE, Kent
TR 2437   f 1924   Covered over in situ

When a large villa was discovered in a beautiful position on the cliff top overlooking the English Channel, part of it had already fallen into the sea and only one mosaic survived. This is a very fragmentary square with a central medallion, contents destroyed, surrounded by four more medallions set across the corners, interspersed with four diamonds, each probably framing a stylised flower or a leaf. The intervening spaces are filled with rectangles of guilloche mat, half stylised flowers and ivy leaves in coiled tendrils. The design is unique in Britain, the nearest equivalent being squares, rectangles and diamonds at Colchester, Essex, Brislington, Somerset and perhaps in Chichester, Sussex.

Illustration Winbolt, S E Roman Folkestone (1925) pls XIV and XV

FOXCOTE, Bucks
SP 7235   4th cent   f 1843   In Queen's Temple, Stowe
A villa with baths had tessellated floors and two mosaics, of which the larger
was lost in an attempt to lift it and a drawing made by the Duke of
Buckingham has also disappeared. The second, a square of guilloche mat
with a border of 'Z' pattern, is on the floor of one of the temples in the
grounds of Stowe School.
Illustration Photograph in Buckinghamshire County Museum, Aylesbury
Reference VCH Buckinghamshire II (1908) 7

FRAMPTON, Dorset
SY 6195   4th cent   Covered over in situ (?)

An 'L' shaped building with rich and varied mosaic floors, more noteworthy
for their interest than for their artistic merit, lies in a meadow beside the
River Frome, not far from the point where Durnovaria's aqueduct drew its
water. The unusual low-lying site and the apparent lack of outbuildings has
led to speculation as to the possibility of this being a place of worship rather
than a villa. The mosaic in Room A was found accidentally in 1794 and a
drawing made by James Engleheart was shown at a meeting of the Society
of Antiquaries of London. Samuel Lysons started excavating the site in 1796
and drew the mosaics, reconstructing the damaged areas of Room A from
Engleheart's illustration. There are interesting similarities in the designs and
motifs employed at Frampton and Hinton St Mary, both in Dorset.
a. (Room A)   f 1794
   A rectangular room with two square mosaics, the smaller, flanked by
panels of peltae, has two interlaced guilloche squares containing a badly
damaged central medallion. The surviving fragment shows a convoluted
smilax or ivy leaf and something which could be a fluted basket, a crown,
a cornucopia or a shell with two leaves. Around the edge of the square
swim sea-beasts and dolphins, one with a pomegranate, which together
with eight-petalled flowers fill the points of the interlaced squares.
   The larger mosaic has one surviving border with two hounds chasing
deer in a forest. The square is cut by guilloche into a grid of nine squares,
five of which contain medallions, that in the centre framing Bacchus with
thyrsus and a bunch of grapes. In the four side panels are Mars in full
armour, holding a spear and plucking a leaf from a tree, Neptune impaling
with his trident a small but aggressive winged sea-beast, Apollo (?)
spearing a python which is coiled round a tree, and finally a disembodied
Jupiter (?) with curly hair and beard, looking down from the sky, as at

Keynsham in Somerset, on a scene of which only two leaves, two flowers and a small square survive. Medallions in each corner panel frame Wind gods, wings in their upstanding red hair, holding conch shells. In every spandrel is a pomegranate with two leaves.

Illustrations RCHM Dorset I (1952) pl 127.1 & Lysons I (1813) iii pl IV

b. (Room B) f 1796

A large room, divided into two unequal parts by short walls, has two mosaics linked by a panel of peltae. The larger floor has an apse, the chord decorated with floral and foliate scroll flanking a Chi-Rho and a band of small chequers, and the remainder inartistically filled with duplex knots and a guilloche mat framing an urn. The square mosaic has an attractive frieze of dolphins springing from the beard of Neptune, who faces the Chi-Rho and breaks into a Latin inscription: 'Neptuni vertex regnem sortiti mobile ventis / scultum cui caerulea e[t froms] delfinis cincta duob [us]', which describes the head of Neptune girt by dolphins. In the frieze of dolphins at the entrance to the other part of the room, Cupid is flanked by two ducks and two marsh birds and by another inscription, badly damaged, '[faci] nus perfici ullum / . . . gnare Cupido'. A central medallion, with a pleated awning border, holds a huntsman (?), on a rearing horse, spearing a wild animal, but as reconstructed by David Neal, it could hold Bellerophon slaying the Chimaera. Of the remaining eight square and semi-circular panels, only two were virtually undamaged and frame unidentified mythological characters. Eight points of a star round the medallion hold small eight-petalled flowers. In the smaller part of the room a square contains a large circle, bordered by guilloche and foliate scroll, framing a fine leopard which is probably looking up at Bacchus, whose cloak is draped over its back. The spandrels have leaf sprays springing from the base of a torch (?), and the square is flanked by two panels, one containing a man with a spear hunting deer, and the other a man confronting an attacking leopard.

Illustrations Smith, D J (1969) pl 3.27, Barley & Hanson (1968) 183 & Lysons I (1813) iii pl V

c. (Room D) f 1796

Heavy coils of guilloche dominate this mosaic and form a central octagon with a god, possibly Jupiter or Neptune, and four surrounding octagons frame Wind gods, with wild red hair, holding conch shells. Lozenges and uneven-sided hexagons, containing some amusing dolphins, are interspersed with plain crosses and 'T' shapes, two of which are chequered.

Illustrations Smith, D J (1969) pl 3.28 & Lysons I (1813) iii pl VII

d. f 1796-7

The three rooms were apparently connected by long meander and swastika pattern corridors, that between Rooms A and D having a guilloche

bordered panel in the centre, but, apart from a fragment of leaf spray in one corner, the contents had been destroyed.
Illustrations BMQ XXXII (1967) 1-2 pl XI & Lysons I (1813) iii pl VI

FROCESTER COURT, Glos
SO 7802   4th cent   f 1961

Excavation of a villa revealed one mosaic floor and small lumps of tesserae which, it has been suggested, may have come from a wall mosaic. Four square panels survived from a long corridor bordered with guilloche, probably formed by the arms of one or more large guilloche swastikas, a pattern which fills at least one square. Next to this is a panel with four concentric squares, and two more hold a duplex knot surrounded by four peltae with leafy tendrils.
Illustration TBGAS LXXXIX (1970) pl II

FROXFIELD see RUDGE FARM

FULLERTON (Wherwell), Hants
SU 3740   4th cent

A villa was first found in 1872, when several mosaics were taken up and re-laid in the hall of Fullerton Manor. Further excavations in 1963 revealed a range of rooms and a corridor. All these mosaics have been drawn by David Neal.

a. f 1872   In Fullerton Manor   plate 2B
   A striking scroll of guilloche bordered circles, with each circle framing a star, borders a square holding a large guilloche bordered medallion cut by guilloche into eight hexagons set round a central octagon. In the centre stands a figure, naked apart from a cloak and helmet, the raised right hand holds a spear and the left hand rests on a shield, indicating that this may be Virtus. Each hexagon frames a Satyr (?), also naked apart from a cloak, and of those surviving, two hold a bill hook, one a tambourine (?) and one a wand. In two spandrels are wreathed busts with no attributes.

b. In Fullerton Manor
   A fragment of black brick pattern on a white ground.

c. In Fullerton Manor
   A fragment of black and white toothed border.

d. Fragments probably formed a square of four plain black swastikas enclosing five square panels, at least one of which frames a duplex knot.

e. In Fullerton Manor
   A rectangle with a broad black border, has two pairs of swastikas enclosing a blank white square with another broad black border.

79

FULLERTON

f. f 1872 In Fullerton Manor
A narrow rectangle or corridor with an all-over peltae pattern which appears to have been laid by two mosaicists, working from opposite ends, who failed to match the pattern when they met! This is probably the pavement described in the *Hampshire Chronicle* of 21 June 1930.

g. f 1872
An unusual mosaic, executed entirely in black and white, has broad bands round a bold dentil border framing a large, but simple labyrinth pattern.
Illustration Photographs of D S Neal's drawings in the Dept of the Environment

FURZEBROOK see EAST CREECH

GADEBRIDGE (Hemel Hempstead), Herts
SP 0508   4th cent   f 1964

A villa with hypocaust and bath house had a number of mosaic pavements. A reconstruction drawing by D S Neal of one of these mosaics shows four large square panels, one filled with guilloche mat, set in an all-over pattern of perspective boxes forming nine stars, and decorated with strange little single spirals, guilloche, duplex knots and ivy leaves.
Reference Britannia II (1971) 110

GATCOMBE, Somerset
ST 5269   In Bristol City Museum

A heavily fortified settlement of 15 to 20 acres has not so far produced any buildings with mosaic or tessellated floors. A fragment depicting a fine fluted urn was presented to the Bristol City Museum in 1946 with no indication as to where or when it was found. It is thought that it may have been discovered at Cambridge Batch, near Gatcombe, where buildings have been recorded, or in the railway cutting at Gatcombe itself, a place which has produced an appreciable amount of Roman material.
Illustration TBGAS LXXXVI (1967) pl XXIV no 6

GAYHURST, Bucks
SP 8546   3rd cent (?)   f 1970

A villa has a coarse tessellated corridor with two plain rectangular panels outlined in red.
Reference Wolverton Historical Journal 2 (1970)

GAYTON THORPE, Norfolk
TF 7318   f 1921

A corridor type villa had two mosaic pavements.
a. (Room I)   Lost
A fragment of one corner shows a guilloche bordered octagon (?).
Illustration Norfolk Archaeology XXIII (1928) pl XIII
b. (Room L)   Lost (?)
Although after its discovery the mosaic was protected by a hut, this was
subsequently used for German prisoners of war and then for hens. A grid
pattern, with the central medallion destroyed, has an ivy leaf in each
spandrel. One corner square has a stylised flower and another an inner
border of ovals, similar to those in the mosaic at Whitton in Suffolk. The
one surviving rectangular panel holds a guilloche bordered lozenge framing
a stylised flower and in each corner, a small curly tendril.
Illustration Norfolk Archaeology XXIII (1928) pl I

GLOUCESTER *(Glevum)*, **Glos**
SO 8318

A *colonia* with defences enclosing an area of 43 acres was laid out in an
uneven grid of streets forming at least 21 *insulae,* and in the course of time
some ribbon development took place beside the roads leading out of the
town. Excavations over the years have produced a great number of mosaic
and tessellated pavements, but records are somewhat sparse and many floors
have vanished without any plans or drawings having been made. Only in very
recent years have a few *insulae* been given numbers.
1. **13-17 Berkeley Street** (Insula I.18)   2nd cent (?)   f 1969
A border of brick pattern outlined in white on a black ground.
Illustration Drawing in City Museum, Gloucester Reference Ant J LII forthcoming
2. **Bon Marché**
This large emporium now covers a number of sites on which mosaics had
been discovered over the years.
a. (Oxbody Inn)   f 1843   Lost
A contemporary newspaper account and a drawing of one corner are all
that survives of this mosaic, which had borders of guilloche and small
triangles and lozenges enclosing hearts and triangles. A little more
information can be gleaned from the following report; 'The colours of
the tesserae forming this pavement were extremely vivid, and the whole
effect in point of brilliancy much heightened by the frequent use of
bright tesserae, approaching to vermilion . . . I traced several other ornaments of the old pattern called the true lover's knot . . . I had not,
however, the satisfaction of seeing the whole uncovered, and only a part
of the centre, which appeared to be extremely beautiful, and of the
same character as those of the corners already described.'
*Illustration JBAA Gloucester (1846) 316 Reference Fullbrook-Leggatt
(1968) 44*

b. (Northgate Street)   2nd or 3rd cent (?)   f 1914   In City Museum, Gloucester
A fine mosaic, now unfortunately thickly coated with yellow varnish, has several borders of plain stripes and one of guilloche enclosing a grid of nine squares and twelve octagons. The square panels are all filled with guilloche mat, apart from the one in the centre which frames a fine urn with leafy tendrils. The octagons hold a variety of stylised flowers, including floral swastikas similar to one found in a mosaic at Caerwent, Monmouthshire, in 1777. The intervening spaces are filled with plain lozenges, duplex knots and panels of guilloche.
Reference Fullbrook-Leggatt (1968) 45   No published illustration
c. f 1934   4th cent
Fragments of mosaic, including a small square panel of guilloche mat, were found here.
Illustration TBGAS LVI (1934) fig 5
d. f 1955   Lost
The corner fragment of a large mosaic has guilloche borders and interlaced guilloche squares containing a medallion with a stylised flower. In the one surviving corner panel is a pelta with tendrils.
Illustration TBGAS LXXX (1961) pl V and VIa
e. f 1958   circa AD 200 (?)   Stored in City Museum, Gloucester
A fragmentary mosaic with an all-over pattern of 'L' shapes in blue on a white ground.
Illustration TBGAS LXXXII (1963) pl IIIa
f. f 1961
Interlaced guilloche squares framing stylised flowers.
Illustration Photograph in City Museum, Gloucester   Reference Fullbrook-Leggatt (1968) 48
3. **Crypt Lane** (Greyfriars)   f circa 1888   Fragment in porch of Friends' Meeting House, Gloucester
Of a fragment of mosaic found under the Meeting House, a local report related 'The remains are said to have been laid as a representation of a male figure with head lying towards the west.' Now only a piece of plain tessellation can be seen.
Reference Fullbrook-Leggatt (1968) 50
4. **Eastgate Street**
a. (Bluecoat School)   f 1806
In rebuilding the Charity School, a coarse mosaic was found lying parallel to the street under what is now the Guildhall.
According to contemporary reports it was divided into panels 'enriched with a great variety of scrolls, frets and other architectural ornaments, and having a wreathed or braided border', together with 'various figures of

fish'. It is not easy to visualise the design and no illustration has been traced.
Reference Fullbrook-Leggatt (1968) 40
b. (National Westminster Bank)   f 1888   Fragment in Bank
A large house with coarse mosaic floors was found in digging foundations for the bank. 'The principal pattern is made of 4 inch squares, alternately white and blue, with wide borders of bands of blue and white. In another compartment the border was a Greek fret.'
Reference PSAL XII 2nd s. (1888) 157
c. (Insula V)   f 1969
  i. Building 18
A fragemnt of scroll.
Illustration Photograph in City Museum, Gloucester Reference Britannia I (1970) 295
  ii. Building 19
A very fragmentary pavement from a room with two mosaics; of one only a border of guilloche remained and of the other several guilloche bordered octagons framing stylised flowers.
Illustration Drawing in City Museum, Gloucester   Reference Britannia I (1970) 295
5. Longsmith Street
a. f 1854   Lost
A large building near the junction with Bull Lane contained several pavements, one of which had a border of interlaced diagonal pattern and was said to have been very beautiful.
References Gents Mag 1854 i 248 & Fullbrook-Leggatt (1968) 52
b. f 1966
Excavations at the east end of the street revealed part of a mosaic pavement composed of a grid of nine squares, one at least framing a stylised flower in a scroll bordered medallion. On one side is a panel of diamonds.
Illustration Photograph of a drawing by D S Neal in the Dept of the Environment   Reference JRS LVII (1967) 195
6. The Market   f 1966-8
During the construction of the Market Hall on the south side of the old Bell Lane, builders' trenches revealed some twenty mosaic floors which were found to have belonged to a series of long narrow stone buildings, built over the remains of the disused Legionary Barracks.
a. Panel in Market Hall, Gloucester
This very fragmentary, but interesting mosaic is composed of an all-over pattern of segmented saltires and interlaced guilloche squares, those in the centre holding a medallion with traces of the figure of Bacchus (?) seated

83

on a leopard. The oblong panels formed by the segmented saltires frame two (?) scrolls of spirals and ivy leaves and two fluted lotus urns with ivy leaves, very like bowls incorporated into a similar pattern in Old Broad Street, London. The arms of the crosses are decorated with twists of guilloche, Greek key swastikas, shaded chequers and ivy leaves. Segmented interlaced squares occupy each corner of the mosaic and in one is a border of convoluted wave crests and a flower bud with leaves. An identical arrangement of this pattern can be found at Tockington Park in Gloucestershire.

Illustration Photograph of a drawing by D. S Neal in the Dept of the Environment   Reference JRS LVII (1967) 194

b. A small corner fragment with an ornamental ivy leaf and perspective boxes.

No published illustration

c. Stored in City Museum, Gloucester
   A fragment of a panel with a stylised flower, the petals formed of hearts and leaves.

No published illustration

7. **Quay Street**   f 1938

A mosaic found outside the city walls, possibly forming the floor of a corridor, has an unusual pattern of diamonds in simple red outline on a blue ground.

Illustration TBGAS LX (1938) pl I

8. **St Mary's Square**   f 1825   Covered over in situ

The church of St Mary de Lode, lying outside the Roman city walls, is said to have been built over several pavements. One was found when workmen were digging foundations for a new nave and was described as follows; 'It was divided into compartments enriched with a variety of scrolls, frets and other ornaments, having a wreathed border enclosing figures of fish and surrounded by guilloche.' An accurate drawing, said to have been made by the architect, now appears to be lost.

References TBGAS LV (1933) 95 & Fullbrook-Leggatt (1968) 58

9. **Southgate Street**

A number of mosaic pavements have been found at various times all along this street, but information is very sparse.

a. f 1746
   A contemporary newspaper reported that 'This week some persons were digging to enlarge a cellar in the Southgate Street . . . they discovered a very curious Roman pavement, done with small stones a little above half an Inch square representing Birds and Beasts in divers colours.'
   References Gloucester Journal 25 March 1746 & Fullbrook-Leggatt (1968) 36

b. f 1904

In the old shop Babyland 'a fine tessellated floor in a very good state of preservation. The tiles were 1¼ inches square, brown and grey, with a castellated pattern round the edge of the floor, in black.'
Reference Fullbrook-Leggatt (1968) 38

10. Westgate Street f before 1850

'Considerable portions of a large tessellated pavement were found, but, unfortunately, almost broken to pieces by the workmen before it was discovered what they were. The *tesserae* were of a blue and white colour, and apparently arranged in a large circular pattern as if for the flooring of a room of considerable size.'
References Clarke, J Architectural History of Gloucester (1850) 6 &
Fullbrook-Leggatt (1968) 42

GRATELEY, Hants

SU 2740

a. f 1910

Fragments of red grid pattern on one side of a floor of rough white tesserae.
Reference PPHFC VI (1907-10) 341

b. f 1915   Illustration displayed in Salisbury & South Wiltshire Museum
Plate 1B

An unusual geometric design based on multiples of four, shows a large guilloche bordered circle within a square (four sides), holding a sixteen-sided figure formed by bands of small traingles; this in turn frames eight panels of guilloche forming an octagon containing a square with a chequered border. In the centre is an attractive shaded circular fan with sixteen ribs.
Illustration PPHFC IX (1920) facing 406

GREAT CASTERTON, Rutland

TF 0009   4th cent   Covered over in situ

A small town with walls and ditches enclosing an area of about 18 acres. To the north-east of this settlement lay a villa in which several fragmentary mosaics were found at some distance from one another.

a. f 1950

A long corridor with a band of large interlaced circles executed in coarse tesserae.
Illustration Corder, P (ed) The Roman Town and Villa at Great Casterton, Rutland First Interim Report (1951) pl Ib

b. f 1952

A fragment showing three most unusual friezes. First a band of hearts, similar to those in panels at Great Staughton in Huntingdonshire, interspersed with small medallions, one containing a Maltese cross; secondly a looped and twisted ribbon and lastly, a frieze of cornucopiae (?) with leaves, very similar to the sprays in the spandrels at Apethorpe in Northamptonshire.

Illustration Corder, P (ed) The Roman Town and Villa at Great Casterton, Rutland Second Interim Report (1954) pls XIIa and XIIIa

c. f 1952

An all-over pattern of perspective boxes forming eight-pointed stars, and framing panels of guilloche, duplex knots and at least one square of pelta-duplex-swastika.

Illustration Corder, P (ed) The Roman Town and Villa at Great Casterton, Rutland Second Interim Report (1954) pls X, XIIb and XIIIb

GREAT CHESTERFORD, Essex
TL5143   f 1847

A small walled town of some 35 acres has so far produced only one house with a plain tessellated floor, but outside the walls a temple was uncovered, which at the time of excavation was thought to be a villa. The ambulatory had a fragment of a guilloche bordered panel at the entrance to the *cella.* Here the floor was paved with red tesserae and had a small square mosaic 'mat' containing a medallion, with one border of stepped triangles, and the contents destroyed.

Illustration Neville, R C Sepulchra Exposita (1848) pls 90, 91 and 93

GREAT STAUGHTON, Hunts
TL 1363   4th cent   f 1958

A small villa with a detached bath house had several very fragmentary mosaic floors.

a. (Room 1)

A very fragmentary mosaic over a hypocaust was reconstructed in a drawing to show a square of perspective boxes, decorated with duplex knots, forming stars and framing a central octagon, possibly containing an urn with leaf sprays. Square panels round the octagon frame shaded interlaced circles and pelta-duplex-swastikas. Small rectangles hold, alternately, small two-coloured triangles and a band of little hearts similar to those at Great Casterton in Rutland.

Illustration Smith, D J (1969) pl 3.25

b. (Room 2)

7 Halstock, Dorset. Saltires and interlaced squares

8A (*above*) Ashcroft Villas, Cirencester. Neptune

8B (*below*) Low Ham, Somerset. Four triple knots

A coarse grey tessellated corridor with two 'mats' of concentric red and white rectangles.
Illustration JRS XLIX (1959) fig 15 (plan)

c. (Room 6)

A very fragmentary mosaic with a border consisting of two rows of pelta-duplex-swastikas and a central square with contents destroyed.
No published illustration

d. (Bath House - Room 2)

The corridor of coarse fawn tesserae has at one end a 'mat' with a simple grid of squares in grey.
Illustration JRS L (1960) fig 26 (plan)

GREAT TEW, Oxon
SP 4027   f 1810

Only part of a villa was excavated and two fragments of mosaic from the bath block were discovered.

a. One fragment shows a panel with a fluted urn and a dolphin, probably one of two flanking the urn.
Illustration Beesley (1848) pl Xa

b. A fragment with two rows of the rare chain pattern, which was also found at Abbots Ann in Hampshire.
Illustration Beesley (1848) pl Xb

GREAT WELDON, Northants
SP 9290   4th cent   f 1738

This villa was re-excavated in 1953 before its final destruction by opencast iron mining, and remains of the corridor mosaic were again uncovered.

a. A square mosaic with lozenges, in simple red outline on a white ground, framing a central square with kite-shaped geometric forms in blue.

b. Perspective boxes, decorated with duplex knots, form a grid, with guilloche mats and pelta-duplex-swastikas filling the squares.

c. A wide corridor with three different designs, the greater part having a border of meander pattern. One length has criss-crossing lines forming squares and triangles, and another an ivy leaf scroll, whilst the third has a much simpler pattern of lozenges and squares in outline.
Illustration VCH Northamptonshire I (1902) fig 22

GREAT WITCOMBE, Glos
SO 8914   f 1818

Very pleasing coloured drawings show the general plan of this large villa and the position of the mosaics in the bath suite. Re-excavations have continued sporadically since 1938 and have revealed a large number of loose tesserae and some pieces of geometric mosaic in the hypocaust of Room 9; fragmentary remains of three mosaic floors may now be seen in situ.

a. (Room 5) Fragments on view in situ (Site Museum)

A complex geometric mosaic is composed of a nine octagon grid, with a central guilloche bordered medallion framing a fluted urn with ivy leaves. The octagons hold medallions with borders of whirling wheel pattern and perspective boxes framing a variety of small stylised flowers, and the whole is bordered by Greek key pattern.

Illustration TBGAS LXXIII (1954) pl VIII

b. (Room 6) On view in situ (Site Museum) plate 15B

A bold swastika border encloses a scatter of sea-beasts, including a sea-cow and a sea-goat, dolphins, fishes, eels and a water flea (?). A broad outer border of red tesserae encloses both the mosaic and a little 'mat' of simple geometric design on the threshold of an adjoining room.

Illustration TBGAS LXXIII (1954) pl VI

c. (Room 10) Fragments on view in situ (Site Museum)

An unusual and simple grid pattern has a large four-pointed star in the central square and a small four-petalled flower in each remaining panel. This room also has a small 'mat' with a saltire in simple outline on the threshold of the next room.

Illustration TBGAS LXXIII (1954) pl VII & Soc of Ant of London Top Colls (Red Port Glos)

GREAT WYMONDLEY (Purwell Mill), Herts
TL 2029 f 1884

A villa with hypocausts and bath buildings was partially excavated, one mosaic being badly drawn in the plan and described as an 'unusual but simple pattern, red, with parallel white lines and gridironed in the centre.'

Illustrations VCH Hertfordshire IV (1914) pl XX (plan) & Transactions of the Hertfordshire Natural History Society IV (1885-7) 43

HACEBY, Lincs
TF 0136 f 1818

Although considerable Roman remains were found, there were only three simple geometric mosaics.

a. A series of plain interlaced octagons, each with a central square.

b. Simple interlaced circles, each with a central square.

c. A chequered diamond within a square panel.

Illustrations Fowler (1796-1818) appendix 2 no 22

HALSTOCK, Dorset
ST 5307   Covered over in situ

John Bellamy's description of a figured mosaic in the *Gentleman's Magazine* of 1818 was, until the re-excavations of 1971, thought to be the only pavement discovered here in the early 19th century. The site was roofed over but, owing to damage by villagers searching for treasure, the building was subsequently pulled down and the floors covered over with bricks and earth. The discovery in 1971 of a mosaic executed in typically Corinian style, but situated in the heart of an area covered by the Durnovarian school, lends special interest to these and future finds in this villa.

a. f 1817   Covered over in situ
'A circular sort of fillet in fretwork goes round, taking off the square of the corners, very nicely and mathematically adjusted; in each of these intermediate spaces is a small circle, each containing the head of a warrior in his helmet, the back of which is represented having a double cross in an oblique position from right to left, extending far over the shoulders; the successive parts inclining to the centre are thrown into squares, and intersected by parallel lines of different colours; these are again divided into lesser squares, leaving a space at right and left, filling up a diamond centre in each square; the centre of the whole is the next part connected with a large mathematical encircled star on one side. This part presents the perfect figure of a face within a circle, very like the rest, with the difference only of being larger, and of a richer construction; the face is ornamented with a sort of irregular ruff or crest round the whole forehead as far as the ears. What sort of device this is I cannot conjecture; if it has an analogy to our Lord's thorny crown on the cross, it is most certainly an aukward *(sic)* representation. Yet we may conclude, from the figures before alluded to having the symbol of the Cross, that this work may have been done during the reign of some of the Christian Emperors . . . '
     This somewhat incoherent description of the mosaic inevitably leads to speculation as to whether the 'double crosses' are Chi-Rhos and whether the central bust with 'an irregular ruff or crest' is similar to the Christ figure at Hinton St Mary.
Reference Gents Mag (1818) i 5

b. (Room 1)   f 1817 (?)   Covered over in situ   plate 7
Re-excavation in 1971 revealed a long narrow mosaic, apparently with a square or rectangular apse on one side, as North Leigh, Oxfordshire. The design is extremely complex, being composed of an all-over pattern of alternate interlaced guilloche squares and saltires, those along the

91

sides being segmented. The saltire nearest to the apse, which may have been drawn by Lysons in 1817 and recently attributed to a site in or near Cirencester in Gloucestershire, has a large stylised flower in the central medallion and a pelta with convolutes decorating each arm of the cross. The other saltires each have a square guilloche panel in the centre, the only one undamaged, framing a small four-petalled flower. The arms are formed of lozenges decorated with ivy leaves, small black and white triangles, shaded chequers and other geometric devices. The interlaced guilloche squares all frame medallions with large stylised flowers, and along the sides are small oblong panels formed by segmented saltires, holding a variety of ivy leaf and lotus bud scrolls. The apse appears to have been filled with parallel bands of guilloche alternating with grey and white stripes. A rectangle of labyrinth pattern forms the threshold to the next room. This mosaic is worth comparing with the pavement found at Old Broad Street, London.

Illustrations Drawing in Soc of Ant of London Top Colls (Red Port Glos) & PDNHAS 93 (1972) figs 10, 11 and 13

(Room 2)   f 1971   Covered over in situ

The small piece of mosaic uncovered so far shows an outer border of little red and grey chequers, in coarse tesserae, running right up to the wall between the two rooms. Within this a piece of sophisticated foliate scroll has two convoluted ivy leaves of a type which also appears in the Venus mosaic at Hemsworth and at Frampton, both in Dorset.

Illustration PDNHAS 93 (1972) fig 12

HARPHAM, Yorks

TA 0863   4th cent   f circa 1904

A villa, partially uncovered in the early 20th century, was further excavated in the 1950's, when some badly damaged tessellated floors were found.

a. A fragment of meander pattern border.

Illustration TERAS XIII ii (1907) fig 7

b. A corridor has broad red longitudinal bands with a hollow square in the centre.

Illustration TERAS XIII ii (1907) fig 7

c. In the City Hall, Hull

Again bold red bands, this time bordering an intricate labyrinth pattern round a tiny stylised flower, which is executed in very small tesserae.

Illustration TERAS XIII ii (1907) fig 7

HARPOLE, Northants

SP 6859   4th cent   f 1846

A rectangular mosaic with an outer border of shaded semi-circles, and a central octagon enclosing a guilloche bordered medallion with a Maltese cross in red on a white ground. The rest of the pavement is divided into four uneven-sided panels, sparsely decorated with semi-circles and lozenges.
Illustration VCH Northamptonshire I (1902) fig 25

HELPSTON, Hunts
TF 1204   f 1827   Lost

Re-excavation in 1967 showed this to have been a large villa, which had a square pavement with borders of striking black and red triangles, large wave crests and guilloche framing a very small panel with an arrangement of linked hearts and lotus flowers, interesting only in its similarity to the central motif of the mosaic found in Lincoln Cathedral. The panel of mosaic now in Helpston Church, and reported in the VCH to have been brought from this site, was probably made from Roman tile and pottery fragments in the 19th century. Further excavations in 1967 revealed five small rooms and a large area of tessellation.
Illustration VCH Northamptonshire I (1902) fig 16

HEMEL HEMPSTEAD see BOXMOOR and GADEBRIDGE

HEMSWORTH, Dorset
ST 9605   4th cent

Several mosaic floors, belonging to a large villa, were found in 1831; they were covered over again and forgotten until more extensive excavations started in 1908, but owing to the shallow covering of soil most of the fifteen pavements had been destroyed by ploughing.
a. Central panel in Dorset County Museum, Dorchester
   The imposing head of a bearded god, barbs issuing from his head, occupies the central panel. Although this would appear to be Jupiter, with lightning flashing behind his head, having been found in the bath suite, it is more likely to be Neptune. The medallion was richly bordered with chevron pattern, wave crests, guilloche and foliate scroll, and in each spandrel were leaf tendrils, possibly springing from an urn.
   Illustrations Toynbee (1964) pl LIXa & photograph in Dorset County Museum, Dorchester
b. In British Museum, London
   A large apse with Venus, much damaged, standing with flowing draperies in front of a scallop shell, a single smilax or ivy leaf with convolutes on either side. The apse has a broad border with a frieze of great dolphins, fishes and shellfish, and fishes also swim in a narrow panel across the

93

chord of the apse, where there is a band of ivy leaves in lozenges.
Illustration BMQ XXXII 1-2 (1967) pl XV

c. In Dorset County Museum, Dorchester
A plunge bath has an effective pattern of black peltae tastefully and
symmetrically arranged on a white ground.
Illustration PDNHAFC XXX (1909) 12

d. Stored in British Museum, London
A corridor with guilloche bordered panels of alternate 'T' shapes and
hourglass triangles, all in black on a white ground, with a band of red
along the sides.
Illustration Hinks (1933) fig 110

e. A border 'of large leaf-shaped ovals 18 inches long, formed of concentric
bands of white, black, blue and red, inclined to one another in pairs at an
angle of 45 degrees and meeting at the points.'
Reference PDNHAFC XXX (1909) 8

HIGH HAM, Somerset
ST 4229   f 1861

Only half a mile from Low Ham, a villa with two mosaic pavements was
found. One was said to have contained rectangular panels with conventional
flowers and leaves inside a cable border, and the other a plain geometric
variation on a key pattern – presumably an all-over swastika pattern.
Drawings, said to be of poor quality and to have been deposited in Somerset
County Museum, Taunton, cannot now be traced.
Reference VCH Somerset I (1906) 328

HIGH WYCOMBE, Bucks
SU 8792   Lost

A mosaic discovered in 1724 led to several further excavations of the villa
before its final destruction in 1955.
a. f 1724
'An old Roman pavement set in curious figures, as circles, squares,
diamond squares, eight squares, hearts, and many other curious figures,
with a beast in the centre, in a circle, like a dog standing sideways by a
tree, all set with stones in red, black, yellow, and white, about ¼ inch
square.' A somewhat incoherent description, but the animal seems reminiscent of the wolf at Aldborough in Yorkshire and the dog (?) at
Cherhill in Wiltshire.
Reference Records of Bucks XVI (1959) 222

b. 2nd cent   f 1862   Illustration displayed in High Wycombe Museum
An early figured mosaic is badly damaged, but enough of the grid pattern

remains to show two rectangles with a guilloche lozenge and single ivy leaves, and probably one with a simple ivy leaf scroll. The one surviving corner square frames what appears to be the bust of a man wearing a helmet and holding a shield, but it has been suggested that this is either a portrait or a figure with wispy hair and wearing a cap. Two flanking panels have a thin frieze of dolphins and two have interlaced eels or sea-beasts.

Illustration Records of Bucks XVI (1959) pl IX

HINTON ST MARY, Dorset
ST 7816   4th cent   f 1963   In British Museum, London

A remarkable mosaic pavement was found when foundations were being dug for extensions to a forge in the village, which with fragments of another pavement belonged to a courtyard villa. A large room is divided by short walls into a square and a rectangle, linked by a panel of peltae. In the square is a guilloche saltire, the central medallion, heavily bordered with guilloche, 'Z' pattern and wave crests, framing what is believed to be a representation of Christ, a Chi-Rho behind His head and a pomegranate on either side. The arms of the cross are decorated with panels of scroll with leaves and tendrils. Each spandrel holds a male bust with upstanding red hair and one wizened arm showing from under his robes; these figures are very similar to the Wind gods at Frampton, but here are possibly intended to be Evangelists, two of them being flanked by pomegranates and two by pomegranate flowers (?). Three of the semi-circles, between the arms of the cross, frame a hound chasing a stag, while the rectangle is divided by guilloche into a square flanked by two panels, both with hounds hunting deer in the forest. In the square is a large medallion, bordered by guilloche and a scroll of leaves and tendrils, framing Bellerophon spearing an impressive Chimaera. In each spandrel is a fluted urn with tendrils.

Illustrations Smith, D J (1969) pl 3.29 & BMQ XXXII (1967) 1-2 pls VI and VIII

HOLCOMBE (Uplyme), Devon
SY 3192   4th cent

Part of a villa, with mosaic and tessellated pavements and a tessellated octagonal plunge bath, was discovered in 1850 and reported lost by 1870. Re-excavation in 1969 revealed a complex bath block, with a room similar to the hexagonal room at Keynsham and the octagonal plunge bath at Lufton, both in Somerset.

a. f 1850   Lost   plate 1A

    A fragmentary, but interesting mosaic with an outer border of swastikas enclosing panels of guilloche, and an ivy leaf scroll springing from an unusual pelta with convolutes. A large guilloche bordered circle encloses six (?) interlaced guilloche bordered medallions, each framing a segmented four-petalled flower, overlaid by a central hexagon with borders of guilloche and wave crest, but with contents destroyed. The one surviving spandrel holds an urn-like lotus bud with small tendrils. This isolated South Devon villa mosaic seems to have more in common with pavements at Littleton and Keynsham in Somerset, than with those so far found in Dorset.

Illustration Soc of Ant of London Top Colls (Red Port Dorset) 5   Reference Arch J XI (1854) 49

b. f 1969

The ambulatory of the beige tessellated octagonal plunge bath revealed fragments of simple blue swastika pattern, a less interesting design than that of the octagonal ambulatory at Lufton in Somerset.

No published illustration   Report in forthcoming volume of TDA

HORKSTOW, Lincs
SE 9819   4th cent   f 1796

a. Fragmentary remains of a large rectangular pavement divided into two squares and one rectangular panel, all three with figured scenes.
i. The first square contains a large guilloche bordered circle with central medallion, from which radiate strands of guilloche, like the spokes of a wheel, dividing the circle into eight segments. Awning pattern borders the medallion, which must have contained the figure of Orpheus, since each segment has a large animal, in procession, separated from another small animal by a pair of peacocks flanking a bunch of grapes. The one remaining spandrel holds a female bust with a small flower or Maltese cross above her shoulder, perhaps one of the Seasons.
ii. A fragmentary second square has a wide border of guilloche mat, containing two large concentric circles held aloft by four giants with legs in the form of serpents. The central roundel had been destroyed, but radiating guilloche spokes divide the circles into four segments, each framing a medallion with naked figures against a dark blue ground. These medallions are flanked by Nereids, Cupids and sea-beasts, all strikingly set on a red ground. The one surviving segment of the inner circle shows dancing children or Cupids holding ribbons attached to a large basket.
iii. In British Museum, London
A dramatic chariot race staged in a *circus,* in which one charioteer is falling from his chariot, having lost a wheel, while another struggles to control his horses as one of them stumbles.

Illustrations Smith, D J (1969) fig 3.2 & Lysons I (1813 i pls I-VI
b. Adjacent to mosaic ii. are fragments of an all-over pattern of black peltae
on a white ground bordered by a band of red.
Illustration Lysons I (1813) i pl VII

HUCCLECOTE, Glos
SO 8717   4th cent   f 1933

A small villa of corridor type, first found in 1910, had simple geometric
mosaics in the south wing. Four rooms had a white grid on a blue ground,
within broad borders of blue and red. In two of the rooms fragments of a
later floor, with a pattern of concentric circles in red, white and brown, lay
six inches above the grid mosaics.
Illustration TBGAS LV (1933) pl X

HURCOT, Somerset
ST 5129   f 1827

Traces of hypocausts, baths and one or two mosaic pavements were found.
A small fragment shows guilloche triangles and the plain borders of a panel.
Illustration Skinner, add. ms 33716 in British Museum, London   Reference
VCH Somerset I (1906) 322

IFOLD, (Painswick), Glos
SO 8510   f 1903

A villa with hypocausts and one very fragmentary mosaic with a broad border
of red and white chequers and interlaced guilloche squares, one framing a
stylised flower in a medallion.
Illustration TBGAS XXVII (1904) fig VI

ILCHESTER *(Lindinis (?))*, Somerset
ST 5222

A number of very small fragments of mosaic and tessellated pavements have
been reported from scattered sites within the walls. Since descriptions are
sparse and mostly limited to the word 'geometric', these mosaics may have
been very simple.
1. **Ivel House**   3rd-early 4th cent (?)   f 1939
A fragment shows borders of plain bands and stepped triangles. Finds of
tessellated and mosaic pavements were also reported from here in the early
18th and the late 19th centuries.
Reference JRS XXX (1940) 174

ILCHESTER

2. Limington Road   2nd-early 3rd cent (?)   f 1950

Borders of blue and white bands and white diamonds on a blue ground and within this a tiny fragment of guilloche (?)

No published illustrations   Reference JRS XLI (1951) 136

ILCHESTER MEAD, Somerset

ST 5122   4th cent   f 1955   Fragments in Yeovil School Museum

A villa lying outside the town walls had one badly damaged mosaic pavement with a panel of peltae pattern along at least one side. What remains of the main area of the floor shows a series of interlaced guilloche squares enclosing medallions, the contents destroyed. In a semi-circle on one side of the mosaic is half a stylised flower and there is an ivy leaf with tendrils in one corner. This is probably another example of the design with four pairs of interlaced squares and a central octagon, which is also found in Cirencester, Gloucestershire, Bignor in Sussex and elsewhere.

Illustration Photographs in Yeovil Museum   Reference SDNQ 27 (1955-60) 80

ILLOGAN, Cornwall

SW 6342   f 1931

A small winged corridor house had coarse tesserae in the corridor, laid in stripes, but not in a pattern.

Illustration JRS XXII (1932) fig 27 (plan)

IPSWICH see WHITTON

ITCHEN ABBAS, Hants

SU 5234   f 1878   Covered over in situ

Three mosaics were found when a villa was partially excavated and a plan was made and shown in JBAA XXXV (1879) facing 209.

a. (Room 1)

A rectangular pavement lying over a hypocaust has a central square framing a medallion, with a large stylised flower and a lotus bud in each spandrel. Two flanking panels contain fluted urns with large tendril scrolls streaming from the handles.

Illustration Morgan (1886) 221

b. (Room 2)

A square mosaic has a wide border of swastikas, enclosing panels of triangles and guilloche, framing a central guilloche mat.

Illustration Morgan (1886) 221

c. (Room 3)   plate 14B

Foliate scroll, guilloche and castellated borders frame a medallion with a female bust, possibly Flora, naked and wearing a wreath of flowers, which stick out all round her head. In the spandrels are two peltae urns with tendrils and two winged peltae.
Illustration JBAA XXXIV (1878) 504

KENCHESTER *(Magnis)*, Herefs
SO 4442

A small fortified Roman town of some 17 acres, with an irregular mesh of streets, along which the houses were built close together.
1. f 1840   Fragment in City Museum, Hereford ·
A pavement described by the excavator, Dr Merewether, as being highly decorated, appears to have had a design of interlaced guilloche squares and panels framing heart arrangements, fish and sea-beasts. Fragments of two other mosaic or tessellated pavements were also found here.
Illustration VCH Herefordshire I (1908) fig 5
2. f 1912   One panel in City Museum, Hereford
A mosaic executed in coarse tesserae has two panels with guilloche octagons, each enclosing a stylised flower within a guilloche bordered medallion.
Illustration Jack (1916) frontispiece
3. f 1912   In City Museum, Hereford
A fragmentary mosaic has swastikas enclosing panels of guilloche and duplex knots bordering a complex all-over pattern of saltires and interlaced guilloche squares, those along the sides being segmented, very similar to mosaics at Old Broad Street in London and Halstock in Dorset. The surviving saltires have central square panels framing guilloche mat, lotus buds and a pelta urn with convolutes, and the arms of the crosses are decorated with lozenges containing various motifs, including shaded chequers and ivy leaves. The interlaced guilloche squares frame stylised flowers with a central duplex knot and a stylised flower with lotus buds and ivy leaf petals. One surviving corner has a small lotus urn.
Illustration Jack (1916) pl 23

KEYNSHAM, Somerset
ST 6469   4th cent (?)   exc 1922   Coloured tracings in Somerset County Museum, Taunton

The first signs of Roman remains were found in 1877, when a graveyard chapel was built, but unfortunately nothing was done and walls and mosaics were destroyed by gravediggers and by the building of the Bath to Bristol road. A great number of pavements from this large and sumptuous villa had already been destroyed before excavations began in the 1920s, but of several

99

enough remained to show they were of particular interest. The mosaicist employed here must have been fascinated by geometric forms, which he used with great skill to create attractive and artistic designs.

a. (North Corridor)

A fragment of swastika pattern enclosing a panel of guilloche.

Illustration Arch LXXV (1926) fig 7

b. (Room A)

A large room, now completely covered by the cemetery chapel, has a fragment of intricate swastika pattern.

Reference Arch LXXV (1926) 114

c. (Room H)

A room, with one side forming a shallow semi-circle, has a rectangular mosaic divided by guilloche into six octagons, each containing a wave crest bordered medallion framing duplex knots and ivy leaves.

Illustration Arch LXXV (1926) pl XII figs 1-2

d. (Room J)   Fragments in Cadbury-Schweppes Somerdale Factory Museum

This fascinating and skilfully designed hexagonal mosaic, unfortunately much damaged, is divided by guilloche into seven hexagons, the one in the centre containing a medallion with a shaded awning pattern border framing a large stylised flower. Each of the six surrounding hexagons holds interlaced guilloche triangles with lozenge swastikas between the points and, in the centre, a wreath of ivy leaves. Round the outer border are six wave crest bordered lozenges containing chequers.

Illustrations Arch LXXV (1926) pls XII fig 2 and XIII figs 1 and 3

e. (Room K)

A panel of spidery foliate scroll, possibly springing from a central urn, divides this mosaic from the last. The floor was very badly damaged, but enough survived to show a most unusual design of three interlaced hourglass circles within a large guilloche bordered medallion. The small central hexagon, formed by the circles, has the remains of a head or mask with wild straggling hair, possibly Medusa, and in the spandrels are a small urn and two triangles. This arrangement of interlaced circles is a more complicated version of that found in the mosaic at Holcombe in Devon.

Illustration Arch LXXV (1926) pl XIII figs 2 and 4

f. (Room L)   Lost

One of two rooms in the shape of a flat-topped triangle had a mosaic executed in coarse tesserae and showing a large two-handled urn flanked by dolphins with red mouths, fins and forked tails. In one corner there was said to be a large heart-shaped leaf with a curved stalk.

Reference Arch LXXV (1926) 122

g. (West Corridor)

An effective all-over pattern with panels of guilloche, peltae and lozenges.

Illustration Arch LXXV (1926) pl XV figs 1 and 5

h. (Room W)   Fragments in Cadbury-Schweppes Somerdale Factory Museum

The largest and most ambitious of all these interesting mosaics, forms a hexagon framing a large circle with a small medallion in the centre, like the hub of a wheel, from which radiate six guilloche spokes. Each of the triangular segments thus formed is cut by the large circle and contains a square panel topped by a semi-circle. On three sides of the floor are rectangular alcoves with plain tesserae and, on two sides, semi-circular alcoves, each containing a band of interlaced circles. The mosaic was unfortunately very badly damaged and the contents of the central medallion had been destroyed. The surviving semi-circles, with rainbow-shaded borders, and the sixteen odd-shaped panels round the outer edge of the hexagon contain a variety of birds with leaf sprays, bare twigs and fruit. A bowl of leaves, leafy sprays, little masks flanked by tendrils, and other geometric devices fill every other nook and cranny, but the main interest lies in the six square panels, bordered alternately by chevrons and 'Z' pattern, of which only the following three survive;

i. A robed figure sits on a high-backed chair, while another starts away as though in horror. Above, and apart from the scene, a bearded man holding a rod, perhaps Jupiter, thoughtfully surveys the scene.

Illustrations Arch LXXV (1926) pl XVI figs 1-2 and XVIII figs 1-2

ii. Jupiter, in the guise of a white bull, lies meekly on the ground feeding from a basket, while Europa, holding the halter, perches nonchalantly on his back. They are presumably about to fly off across the sea to Crete, a chapter in the saga which may be seen in the mosaic at Lullingstone in Kent.

Illustration Arch LXXV (1926) pl XVII fig 1

iii. The upper half of the panel is much damaged, but two figures can be distinguished, one with double pipes and the other with a tambourine, dancing round a severed head in a Phrygian cap, pipes still between the lips. This is perhaps intended to be the head of Orpheus as it floats away down the river, here portrayed playing on pipes due to the difficulty, under the circumstances, of showing him playing his lyre.

Illustration Arch LXXV (1926) pl XVII fig 2

KING'S WESTON, Glos

ST 5377   3rd cent   f 1948

A villa, found on a site overlooking the Severn Estuary near Bristol, was partially excavated and preserved in situ. A mosaic from Brislington has been laid in one of the rooms.

a. (Room III)   On view in situ (Site Museum)
A small square of guilloche mat similar to Room 3 at Woodchester.
Illustration TBGAS LXIX (1950) pl IIIa

b. (Room IV)
A vestibule has two adjacent guilloche bordered panals, each framing a simple four-petalled flower.
Illustration The Roman Buildings at King's Weston Park (Bristol City Museum Publication 1957) pl I

c. (Room VII)   On view in situ (Site Museum)
A large square with plain borders is flanked by two panels, one has a large urn with unusual fluting and two tightly spiralled tendrils flowing from the base, and the other chevron bordered medallions framing stylised flowers. The square has five guilloche or chevron bordered medallions containing very simple flowers and linked by four eight-pointed 'shields'. A narrow panel leading to the next room has a strip of simple scroll pattern.
Illustration TBGAS LXIX (1950) pls IVb, V and VI

KIRK SINK (Gargrave), Yorks
SD 9353   3rd cent   f 1969

Two adjacent buildings with heated rooms and mosaic floors were found here.
Reference Britannia I (1970) 280

LANDWADE (Exning), Suffolk
TL 6167   4th cent   f 1904   Fragment in Museum of Archaeology, Cambridge

The dining room of a villa, rebuilt in stone in the 3rd century, had an unusual pavement of red tesserae with a large semi-circle, bordered by guilloche and triangles, set in the middle of the floor as a focal point for the diners reclining on their couches round the semi-circle.
Reference JRS L (1960) 228 and fig 29

LATIMER, Bucks
SU 9998   f 1864

This large villa was partially excavated several times before the systematic excavations of 1964-71, when traces of the remains of mosaics and a few fragmentary pavements were found.

a. (Room 27)   2nd cent
A very small fragment of geometric pattern in black on a white ground.
Illustration Branigan (1971) pl V

b. (Room 22)   3rd cent
All that survived of a square (?) mosaic was one border consisting of a

band of black diamonds on a white ground.
Illustration Branigan (1971) pl VI

c. (Room 33)   Early 4th cent
Fragments of borders of guilloche, wave crests, and a swastika pattern with
alternate strands of black and red similar to the swastikas at Combley on
the Isle of Wight.
Illustration Branigan (1971) pl IX

LEA CROSS (Pontesbury), Salop
SJ 4108   f 1793   Lost

A villa built on marshy ground had the most sophisticated mosaic so far
discovered in Shropshire. Within a plain square, a large circle of guilloche
encloses a central cushion-shaped panel containing a stylised flower and ivy
leaves. Ellipses on four sides of the 'cushion' frame strange truncated scallop
shells and in each spandrel is a fluted lotus urn, with tendril handles, which,
lacking a central petal, look more like urns than flowers.
Illustration VCH Shropshire (1908) fig 34

LEICESTER *(Ratae Coritanorum)*, Leics
SK 5804

A *civitas* capital of some 105 acres must have had numerous rich houses,
judging by the quality of the mosaics discovered here, whereas the surrounding countryside has so far produced no wealthy villas. Of the many mosaics
and tessellated pavements found over the years, some now lie in the disused
Central Railway Station in Leicester, where they are ate present unfortunately
inaccessible to the public.
1. **All Saints Church**   f circa 1675   In Jewry Wall Museum, Leicester
An octagonal panel from a larger pavement depicts Cyparissus caressing his
tame stag, with Cupid preparing to shoot an arrow from his bow.
Illustration VCH Leicestershire I (1907) pl III
2. **Blackfriars Street**
a. f 1754   Lost
Three nine foot square mosaics, with guilloche borders round geometric
designs, could be panels from a corridor, although they are rather large for
this purpose.
  i. An effective pattern of pelta-duplex-swastikas.
Illustration Arch J LXXV (1918) pl VIII
  ii. Interlaced circles, each enclosing a small square.
Illustration VCH Leicestershire I (1907) pl IV
  iii. An all-over swastika pattern enclosing five duplex knots.
Illustration VCH Leicestershire I (1907) pl V

A drawing at the Society of Antiquaries of London showing part of two adjacent panels of interlaced circles and an all-over swastika pattern with no duplex knots, may be of two more corridor panels or of another version of ii and iii above.

Illustration Drawing in Soc of Ant of London Top Colls (Red Port Leics) II

b. f 1830   2nd cent (?)   In Old Central Station, Leicester

A striking and very sophisticated example of a guilloche bordered nine octagon grid, with outer borders of ivy leaf and lotus flower scroll. The central octagon frames a simple square of guilloche mat within a guilloche bordered medallion, and in each corner is a circle with two variations of a kind of shaded scale pattern; one with a central flower and radiating lines bisecting small shaded interlaced circles, similar to a medallion at West Dean, Hampshire; the other with a central duplex knot and large intersecting circles forming small triangular scales. The remaining four octagons all have a central stylised flower, two with wave crest borders and two (?) with a beautiful naturalistic floral and foliate scroll. Small squares between the octagons frame stylised flowers, one a floral swastika.

Illustration VCH Leicestershire I (1907) pl III

3. Blue Boar Lane   2nd cent (?)   f 1958   Fragments in Jewry Wall Museum, Leicester

A number of tessellated pavements and two small fragments of mosaic were found, one with a bold swastika pattern and the other with small geometric panels.

No published illustration   Reference TLAHS 35 (1959) 79

4. High Cross Street   (Coffee House)   f 1901   In Old Central Station, Leicester

A fragment with an all-over pattern of duplex knots bordered by chequers and guilloche.

Illustration VCH Leicestershire I (1907) pl VII

5. Norfolk Street (Dannet's Hall Orchard)

A villa with a number of simple geometric mosaics was found outside the town walls; the owner may have been connected with the nearby quarries.

Reference Arch J XLVI (1889) 52

a. f 1782

A long corridor with adjacent panels of interlaced circles and octagons bordered by bands of small chequers.

Illustration Gents Mag 1786 ii pl I

b. f circa 1850   In Jewry Wall Museum, Leicester

The mosaic laid in a large room was totally destroyed, but the apse, holding a crudely executed fluted scallop shell flanked by two dolphins with borders of guilloche and stepped triangles, survived.

Reference Arch J XLVI (1889) 54 & VCH Leicestershire I (1907) 197

9A (*above*) Downton, Wiltshire. Urn with fish handles

9B (*below*) Little Minster Street, Winchester. Saltires and interlaced squares

10B Bignor, Sussex (Room 3). Venus and gladiators. (From Samuel Lysons, *Reliquiae Britannico-Romanae* III, 1817, plate XVI)

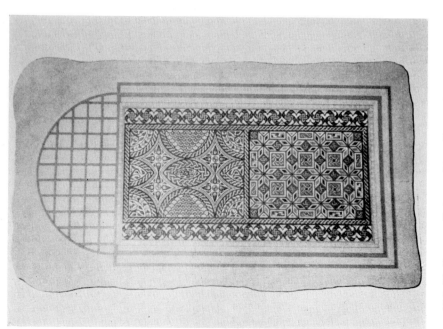

10A Medbourne, Leicestershire. Geometric pavement with apse. (From coloured lithograph in the Society of Antiquaries of London)

6. Ruding Street   f 1896   In Old Central Station, Leicester
Fragments of chequer pattern in two shades of red.
Reference Leicester Daily Post 14 August 1900

7. 50 & 52 St Nicholas Street   2nd cent   f 1898   In Jewry Wall Museum, Leicester
The three mosaic pavements found here were preserved in situ until 1965, when they were moved to the Museum.

a. A very attractive nine octagon grid, with a central guilloche bordered medallion framing a beautiful peacock in full display, but unfortunately badly damaged; although there are many peacocks in British mosaics, this is the only one shown with its tail outspread. The remaining octagons frame stylised flowers within borders of guilloche, wave crests and triangles, and perspective boxes decorated with small flowers and duplex knots. The outer border is of ivy leaf and lotus flower scroll. This mosaic has much in common not only with the one found in Blackfriars Street, Leicester, but also with Room 5 at Great Witcombe in Gloucestershire.
Illustration VCH Leicestershire I (1907) pl I

b. An oblong mosaic with a rectangular panel of 'L' shapes and squares in grey and white forming a simple diagonal pattern. The remaining area of the floor is dotted with clusters of fine white tesserae arranged to form crosses, a feature reminiscent of a border design at Fishbourne in Sussex.
Illustration Gents Mag 1898 i fig 2

8. Vine Street   2nd cent   f 1839   Fragments in Old Central Station, Leicester.
A fragmentary mosaic with a large guilloche saltire, the central roundel destroyed, and at least one arm decorated with a stylised flower. In the semi-circles are ivy leaf sprays and a fluted urn occupies each of two surviving corners.
Illustration VCH Leicestershire I (1907) pl V

9. 'Near the town of Leicester'   f 1612
At an unspecified location a floor was found 'wrought in mosaic work of stone and divers colours representing flowers, knots, birds, fretts etc.'
Reference Nichols, J. History and Antiquities of the County of Leicester I (1795) 9

LENTHAY, Dorset
ST 6215   f 1836   On view at Sherborne Castle

The mosaic found beside the railway line near Sherborne was lifted without any further excavation, although it was said to have been only the central portion of a pavement with rich borders. Within interlaced guilloche squares, the naked figures of Apollo, seated on a rock and playing on his lyre, and Marsyas, dancing to a double flute, are engaged in a deadly musical

contest. Although the theme is classical and the scene lively and gay, the figures are crudely executed.
Illustration Smith, D J (1969) pl 3.31

LINCOLN *(Lindum)*, Lincs
SK 9771

A *colonia* founded on this spot had fortifications enclosing an area of 41 acres, but subsequently, as the town expanded, the defences were extended to enclose about 97 acres. Most of the mosaic and tessellated pavements have been found on the site of the earlier town, but there is usually little more than a brief reference to their discovery.

1. Bailgate
In the 19th century a plain white tessellated pavement was found during the rebuilding of St Paul's Church, also a floor of black and red tesserae near St Paul's Lane, and several pieces of mosaic while building a school near the Mint Wall.
a. (Mint Wall)   f 1897   In Lincoln City Museum
   A fragmentary corner shows a guilloche bordered medallion holding a bust with a cornucopia and a crown of corn ears (?), possibly one of the Seasons; in the spandrels are lotus flowers and hearts.
   Illustration Lincoln Museum Postcard   Reference Toynbee (1964) 282
b. (Wesleyan Methodist Chapel)   f 1878-9
   'Pavement recently found at east end of New Wesleyan Chapel about 40 yards east from centre of road leading up to Newport Gate.' A drawing beside this report shows a guilloche bordered semi-circle framing a spray of ivy leaves, which is possibly a panel between the arms of a saltire.
   Illustration JBAA XXXV (1879) facing 308

2. The Castle   f 1846   Lost
In 1786 'two handsome pavements' were found and a rough plan of the floors was made, but of a later find a good drawing exists. A large circle within a square holds two interlaced guilloche squares framing a stylised flower composed of eight heart-shaped petals. In the spandrels are tall, ornately decorated urns with trailing leaf tendrils. In each of two flanking rectangular panels is a semi-circle with an elaborate urn and two quarter-circles with ivy leaves and tendrils, which also decorate the intervening spaces.
Illustration Whitwell (1970) pl III

3. Cathedral Cloisters   f 1793
a. Fragment in Lincoln Cathedral
   An attractive mosaic with perspective boxes forming four large stars, which frame a central square with a curious arrangement of linked hearts and lotus flowers, identical to the central motif at Helpston in

Huntingdonshire. The perspective boxes are decorated with lotus buds and ivy leaves and hearts. The pavement is bordered by broad black and white bands.
Illustration Fowler (1796-1818) no 4

b. A corridor with broad borders of red and white, running from the room described above, and panels of lozenges, triangles and pairs of peltae forming circles.
Illustration Fowler (1796-1818) no 4

4. Exchequergate   f 1879   Fragment in Lincoln City Museum
A large guilloche bordered saltire lies within a border of Greek key pattern, the central medallion holding an eight-pointed star and the arms of the cross being decorated with four-petalled stylised flowers. In the semi-circles are dolphins and in each corner a shaded heart.
Illustration Morgan (1886) 138

5. Monson Street   f 1845   Lost
Numerous pavements were recorded east of the High Street Unitarian Chapel, indicating the presence of a large villa beside the road leading south-wards out of the town. One is described as being a fine square mosaic,
' . . . the centre is destroyed; eight rays proceeded from it, forming a star-like figure; around this a circular guilloche border of dark grey and two shades of red and white tesserae placed within a square, the angles of which are filled in with shaded heart-shaped figures.'
Reference Arch J XVII (1860) 16

6. Greetwell Fields   f circa 1884   Fragments in Lincoln City Museum
The owner of this villa, which lay outside the Roman city walls, may well have been involved in iron working, which is still carried on in this area and which led to the uncovering of the mosaics over the years from 1884 to 1893, and then to the final destruction of the site.

a. (Room A)
A plunge bath with tessellated walls.

b. (Rooms D, E & F)
Three narrow rooms with variations on a design of concentric rectangles and stripes.

c. (Corridor G)
A very long north to south corridor with a single row of blue swastikas running its full length.

d. (Corridor H)
Another even longer corridor, lying east to west at right angles to the last, has a pattern of chequers.

e. (Room J)
A strange mosaic with broad red and white stripes, and in the centre a square of white bordered with blue.

f. A long corridor, together with the others probably enclosing three sides of a courtyard, has a great variety of geometric patterns in square guilloche panels; these include urns, pelta-duplex-swastikas, eight-pointed stars and lotus buds. A scroll of guilloche bordered circles frames flowers, duplex knots and peltae.

Illustrations Arch J XLIX (1892) 260 & ms plan and drawing by Quarry Manager Ramsden (1893) in Lincoln City Museum

LITTLECOTE PARK (Ramsbury), Wilts

SU 2970   4th cent   f 1730   Lost   Needlework copy on view at Littlecote

A very sophisticated mosaic floor is divided into two parts by a panel of chevron pattern. One half has a wide chequered border and a large square of swastika pattern framing four guilloche bordered panels with stylised flowers. A rectangular panel at one end has a central urn flanked by two sea-beasts, dolphins and shellfish, and at the other end an urn with drooping sprays of leaves flanked by two proud-looking black panthers.

The other half of the room is square with a large circle divided into four segments by guilloche running from a central medallion. In the centre stands Orpheus with his lyre, and in each segment is a woman riding on a beast, perhaps representing the four Seasons. The first on a hind (?) is naked and holding a mirror, the second on a panther naked and holding a bird, the third on a cow (?) robed and holding a leafy twig, and the last on a goat (?) is also robed. In each spandrel is a large lotus flower. There is an apse on each of three sides, two linked to the main part of the floor by an oblong panel of interlaced circles and bordered by tendril scroll, and all three holding a large scallop shell or fan with a little face on the hinge.

Illustration Smith, D J (1969) pl 3.16

LITTLETON, Somerset

ST 4931   4th cent   Lost

A courtyard villa, partially excavated in 1827 and again in the 1950s, had a long corridor and four rooms paved with good mosaics, all badly damaged.

a. In 1827 the *Gentleman's Magazine* reported that a mosaic had 'a male figure in its centre, supposed to be a Bacchus, surrounded by an arabesque border of foliage.'

Reference Gents Mag 1827 ii 113

b. Another pavement was said to have been 'surrounded by an à la Grecque border, and in the centre three letters only remained visible, viz., FLA . . .', perhaps the artist's signature.

Illustration VCH Somerset I (1906) fig 81 (plan)

c. f 1951

A large fragment shows an outer border of swastika pattern and a guilloche bordered square enclosing a large medallion with six (?) concentric interlaced guilloche circles. In the centre of one of these are ivy leaf tendrils, and a 'Z' and guilloche bordered medallion occupies one of the spandrels. The central medallion was probably the same shape as that in the centre of Room K at Keynsham.

Illustration Drawing on view in Somerset County Museum, Taunton
Reference PSANHS XCVI (1951) 44

LLANFRYNACH, Brecon
SO 0625   4th cent   f 1784

A villa was found in the Usk Valley, some miles downstream from the Roman fort of Y Gaer, near Brecon. Partial excavation revealed a bath block with four mosaic floors and a distinct similarity in style can be found between ·these mosaics and those in the temple complex at Lydney in Gloucestershire.
a. (Room 2)
   A series of bold concentric squares in two colours frame a central guilloche bordered panel of guilloche mat.
b. (Room 4)
   A damaged mosaic with the entwined tails of sea-beasts (?), a fish and a sea shell.
c. (Room 7)
   A rectangle of large and small blue chequers, arranged in diagonal lines, forming white 'L' shapes.
d. (Room 8)
   A long narrow pavement divided into two panels by plain bands; the larger part has a peltae pattern and the smaller a curious design, looking like wings, but possibly intended to be a scallop shell.
   Illustrations Arch VII (1785) pl XVII & BBCS XIII (1949) fig 1

LLANTWIT MAJOR, Glam
SS 9569   4th cent   f 1888

A large and isolated courtyard villa, lying within an earthen enclosure, had been partially cleared in 1888 and re-excavated in 1938, two mosaics being uncovered on each occasion.
a. (Room 8)
   A mosaic very similar to one found at the Bon Marché site in Gloucester, has a grid of squares and octagons. The octagons hold medallions framing a variety of stylised flowers, including at least one with lotus flower and ivy leaf petals and another with a duplex knot backed by four peltae and leaves, a form which may also be found in mosaics on several scattered

sites in Britain. The squares hold stylised flowers and guilloche mat, and lozenges in the intervening spaces are decorated with ivy leaves and shaded chequers.

Illustration Arch Camb CII (1953) pl IV 2

b. (Room 9)
Only a fragment survived to show a guilloche border and a panel of blue swastika pattern on a white ground linking this room to the last.

Illustration Arch Camb CII (1953) pl V 1

LONDON *(Londinium)*
TQ 3281

The Roman city of *Londinium* grew and flourished on the Thames estuary, where it was well placed for the Continental sea trade. It was the centre of the British road system and the capital.

During the Boudiccan revolt of AD 60-1, when the town was virtually defenceless, it was raided and burnt to the ground; subsequently being rebuilt to cover approximately 330 acres, and of the numerous public buildings which must have existed, parts of the forum-basilica and the governor's palace (?) have been discovered. A temple dedicated to the oriental mystery cult of Mithras, a strong rival to Christianity, was found in 1954. The houses of wealthy merchants appear to have been built in the valley of the Walbrook, a small tributary of the Thames, and it is here that a number of good mosaic pavements have been found, including those from Bucklersbury and the Bank of England.

A great many plain tessellated pavements and small fragments of mosaics have been discovered over the years, but since the city has been occupied continuously from Roman times, few have been found undamaged. Some were recorded, but not illustrated, before their destruction. Several plain tessellated pavements have been preserved on the north side of the Church of St Vedast in Foster Lane, in the crypt of St Brides Church in Fleet Street, in All Hallows, Barking Church and in the Royal Bank of Canada.

1. Bank of England
a. 3rd cent (?)   f 1805   In British Museum
A small guilloche bordered square holds an acanthus leaf cross in a plain circle, with lotus flower urns in the spandrels.

Illustration RCHM London III (1928) pl 47

b. 2nd-3rd cent (?)   f 1923   In Bank of England
Fragments of a square with an outer border of swastikas, a central medallion and an ivy leaf in each spandrel.

Illustration Merrifield (1965) pl 69

c. 2nd-3rd cent (?)   f 1934   In Bank of England

Four square guilloche bordered panels each hold a stylised flower.
Illustration Merrifield (1965) pl 68

2. Bartholomew Lane   f 1841

A fragment with a scroll of ivy leaves in black on a white ground
Reference Merrifield (1965) no 181

3. Birchin Lane   f 1857   In Guildhall Museum

A fragment with a lively sea-beast.
Reference Merrifield (1965) no 209

4. Bishopsgate Street   f 1839

A fragment of perspective box pattern forming a star.
Illustration RCHM London III (1928) fig 30

5. Crosby Square

a.   f circa 1908   In Guildhall Museum

A fragment of two guilloche bordered panels.
Reference Merrifield (1965) no 325

b.   f 1908   In Crosby Hall, Chelsea

A fragment of ivy leaf scroll.
Illustration Merrifield (1965) pl 71

6. Fenchurch Street   f 1857   In British Museum

A fragment with a rectangular panel containing an urn and a brightly
coloured peacock, almost certainly one of a pair flanking the urn.
Illustration RCHM London III (1928) pl 40

7. Finch Lane (Cornhill)   f circa 1844   In London Museum

A small fragment shows the crudely executed bust of a woman with a toothy
smile.
Illustration Merrifield (1965) pl 70

8. Foster Lane   f circa 1877   Stored in London Museum

A fragment with a panel of guilloche
Illustration London in Roman Times pl Xb

9. 11 Ironmonger Lane   f 1949   On view in situ (with permission)

A fragment with a grid of hexagons enclosing stylised flowers and one
swastika lozenge.
Illustration Merrifield (1965) pl 67

10. King William Street   f 1920   In London Museum

Two fragments, one plain and the other with a guilloche border.
Reference London in Roman Times 39

11. Leadenhall Street

a.   f 1803   Fragments in British Museum

A square mosaic with an outer border of duplex knots framed in diamonds,
and peltae with octopus-like tentacles and lotus bud tips. A central
medallion, with borders of awning, wave crest and shaded wave patterns,
holds a portly and soulful Bacchus, his wreath and cloak ornamented with

113

glass tesserae, reclining on the back of a fine tiger. In the spandrels are two urns and two pelta urns, all wreathed in tendrils, leaves and flowers.
Illustration RCHM London III (1928) pl 49

b. f 1863   3rd cent   In British Museum
Two interlaced guilloche bordered squares form an octagon containing a graceful foliate cross with a circular fan motif in the centre, and a fan in each corner of the mosaic.
Illustration Hinks (1933) fig 94

12. Mansion House Street   f 1867   Lost
A drawing of the mosaic, now apparently lost, showed it to have been 'a mosaic of good execution, both in design and treatment. It comprised a square enclosing a circle; the central ornament was a vase . . . the *tessellae* composing it were formed of brown, white, red and black materials, with the addition of bright green glass; around the vase there appeared portions of a tree with foliage; also an object resembling an archway, with embattled figures and other objects, the meaning and intention of which it is difficult to describe without an illustration. Around the whole were two simple bands of black *tessellae*, separating the circle from an elaborate scroll of foliage and flowers analogous in character to that on one of the pavements at Bignor. At each corner was a rose or other flower, showing eight petals in stones of white, black, and varied colours. From the centre of each flower there spring in opposite directions two branches, which unite with a leaf, possibly that of the lotus, and of analogous form to that observed within the scroll.'
Reference Morgan (1886) 193

13. Old Broad Street   f 1854   Lost
A large square pavement has an all-over pattern of saltires and interlaced guilloche squares, bordered by an attractive wreath of lotus flowers and leaves. The square central panels of the saltires frame fluted urns and in the middle of the mosaic, either a Bacchante riding on a leopard or Europa on a white bull. The arms of the crosses are richly decorated with duplex knots, leaves, shaded chequers, swastikas, lotus flowers and various geometric devices. The interlaced squares hold medallions with stylised flowers formed of ivy leaves and lotus buds, and 'sunflowers' with central duplex knots. The segmented interlaced squares round the edges of the pavement frame scallop shells and fluted bowls with leaves and flowers.
Illustrations RCHM London III (1928) pls 39 and 48 & alternative version VCH London I (1909) pl 48

14. Paternoster Row   f circa 1840   Lost
A large mosaic with a border of guilloche enclosing rosettes round panels with birds and beasts and an object said to resemble a starfish.
Reference Arch XXIX (1842) 155

15. Queen Victoria Street (Bucklersbury)   f 1869   In Guildhall Library

Bookstore
A large apsed pavement has two interlaced squares framing a stylised flower within awning pattern and guilloche borders, and in each corner is a stylised flower or leaf spray. Leading to the apse is a broad panel with a central pelta urn from which spring flowers and a striking scroll of leaves and berries. The apse is heavily bordered by guilloche, enclosing a semi-circle of shaded scale pattern and a scallop shell.
Illustration Merrifield (1965) pl 65

16. St Paul's Churchyard   f 1841   Lost
A mosaic with a pattern of rosettes on a white ground.
Reference Arch XXIX (1842) 272

17. Suffolk Lane   f 1969   In Guildhall Museum
A small fragment of a panel bordered by stepped triangles, probably coming from a floor in a large official building.
No published illustration Reference Britannia I (1970) 292

18. Threadneedle Street   f 1841   Stored in British Museum
a. A corridor with an ingenious arrangement of lozenge swastikas and squares containing small stylised flowers and duplex knots.
   Illustration RCHM London III (1928) pl 50a
b. A corridor with borders of meander pattern and a square panel framing an ornate and many-petalled stylised flower, the inner ring of petals being composed of trefoils.
   Illustration RCHM London III (1928) pl 50b

19. Southwark, S.E.1.   TQ 3280
A number of tessellated pavements have been found near the Roman road leading to a crossing of the River Thames.
a. f 1658
   A mosaic said to have been found somewhere south of Winchester House, was described as being 'wrought in various colours; and in the midst thereof, betwixt curtain borders in the fashion of wreathed columns, the form of a serpent very lively expressed in that kind of Mosaic work.'
   Reference Gents Mag 1815 i 225
b. St Saviour's Church   f 1832   Fragment in Southwark Cathedral
   A red tessellated corridor was found in the churchyard,
   possibly belonging to a building with walls running under the choir of the church.
   Reference Etymology of Southwark (1839) 5

LOW HAM, Somerset
ST 4328   4th cent   f 1946

A large villa had a number of particularly interesting mosaic pavements.

a. In Somerset County Museum, Taunton
This remarkable mosaic, found in the bath suite, lacked the plain
tessellated surround from which the patterned area of the mosaic can
usually be viewed. In countries bordering the Mediterranean such mosaics
had an external ambulatory, which suggests that the following scenes from
Virgil's *Aeneid* may have been laid by a travelling mosaicist, perhaps from
North Africa.

Scene 1   The four leading characters are presented. Venus, naked save
for a diadem and a fourfold breast and back chain (also worn by the Three
Graces in a North African mosaic), leans affectionately on the shoulders of
her son, Cupid, who disguised as Ascanius son of Aeneas, is sent by Venus
to kindle the fires of love between Aeneas and Dido. Aeneas, bearded and
cloaked, leans on his spear and glances at a pensive Dido. Both stand
awkwardly, with legs crossed.

Scene 2   A long side panel shows the arrival of the Trojan fleet at
Carthage; in the middle boat sits Ascanius wearing a Phrygian cap, and in
the stern is what is though to be the Palladium. In the leading boat a
member of the crew hands a present for Dido to Achates, faithful friend of
Aeneas.

Scene 3   Aeneas and Dido are out hunting with Ascanius/Cupid.

Scene 4   Sheltering from a storm beneath the trees, Aeneas clasps Dido
in his arms at the climax of their love affair.

Scene 5   The central and final scene shows Venus, her little game ended
by Jupiter, who has instructed Aeneas to leave Carthage and set sail for
Italy. Two cupids represent the fate of the lovers. One, with eyes closed
and torch hanging down, tells of Dido's despair and suicide, while the
other, vigorous and joyful with torch aloft, heralds the triumphant completion of Aeneas' mission, the founding of Rome.

Illustrations Smith, D J (1969) pl 3.5 & Toynbee (1963) figs 235 and 259

b. In Somerset County Museum, Taunton
Leading directly from the last room is a mosaic with a large guilloche
bordered circle enclosing two interlaced guilloche squares; these frame a
medallion with four lotus buds and four leaves in the form of a double
cross.

*Illustration Ralegh Radford, C A & Dewar, H S L   The Roman Mosaics
from Low Ham & East Coker (Somerset County Museum Publications
1954) 2*

c. Covered over in situ   plate 8B
An alcove leading off a plain tessellated corridor has a roughly executed
mosaic with a large guilloche bordered medallion holding a unique
arrangement of four triple knots.

Reference SDNQ XXV (1950) 62

d. Covered over in situ
A rectangular mosaic with a simple and effective all-over pattern of
swastikas enclosing panels with five small squares.
No published illustration   Reference SDNQ XXV (1950) 62
e. Lost
Finely executed fragments of a mosaic over a hypocaust showed fishes and
a piece of foliate scroll.
No published illustration   Reference SDNQ XXV (1950) 62
f. Covered over in situ
Plain concentric rectangles.
No published illustration

LUFTON, Somerset
ST 5117   4th cent   Covered over in situ

Excavations during the 1940s and 1950s revealed an unpretentious villa with
a relatively large and luxurious bath block and a number of mosaic and
tessellated floors.
a. (Corridor 1)
A simple floor of coarse grey tesserae with red stripes and a panel of
smaller tesserae at the entrance (?) to Room 2.
*Illustration Photograph in Wyndham Museum, Yeovil   Reference PSANHS
XCVII (1952) 94*
b. (Room 2)
Fragments show a simple guilloche saltire, the arms probably radiating
from a central medallion. In plain rectangular panels between the arms
are two urns, one without handles, both being flanked by a series of
triangles. There were, presumably, two more urns in a similar position
on the other two sides of the pavement.
*Illustration Photograph in Wyndham Museum, Yeovil   Reference PSANHS
XCVII (1952) 96*
c. (Room 4)
A badly damaged mosaic has a panel of peltae pattern, and interlaced
rectangles bordered by coarse grey tesserae with a red stripe.
No published illustration   Reference PSANHS XCVII (1952) 96
d. (Room 13)
The cold room floor was badly damaged, but enough remained to show
that it had been divided into two squares, apparently separated by a strip
of six small panels, the contents of which had unfortunately been destroyed. Each square held a different form of saltire, the larger being the
more complex in design, but very little survived. The central medallion
was lost, apart from a fragment which, with a stretch of the imagination,

could be said to show a lobster claw in the head of Neptune. On each of the arms of the cross was a rainbow bordered medalliòn, two hold busts, one of a muscular young man, possibly an athlete. Interlaced guilloche squares between the arms of the cross each frame an urn with trailing leaves. Along one side of the floor there had been a scroll of guilloche bordered circles framing small stylised flowers. The smaller saltire was also badly damaged, but at least two of the arms are decorated with a duplex knot and a flower. Sprays of leaves and half a stylised flower fill the semi-circles between the arms of the cross, and an unusual little spray of leaves occupies the only surviving corner of the square.

Illustrations PSANHS XCVII (1952) fig 3 (plan) and pl V & photograph in Wyndham Museum, Yeovil

e. (Room 14)

A large octagonal plunge bath, paved with red tiles, has a remarkable mosaic floored ambulatory, with a more sophisticated design than that in the octagonal ambulatory at Holcombe in Devon. Seven narrow panels with heavy borders of guilloche contain an assortment of fish, some blowing bubbles and some with eels twined round them. The eighth panel, leading to Room 15, has a small bowl of fruit (?) flanked by duplex knots, but here the mosaicist seems to have run into difficulties. Having executed a rainbow-shaded wedge and a small duplex knot with lotus flowers in the corners, he found the bowl was not in the centre of the panel and therefore the next duplex knot and the wedge had to be larger and he omitted the lotus flower and the rainbow shading.

Illustration PSANHS XCII (1946) pl IV & XCVII (1952) pls VI-IX and X i

f. (Room 15)

A small square room, opening off the ambulatory, has a large octagon with borders of guilloche and of little lozenges, which are quite unique in Britain, and a large stylised flower lies in the central medallion. There is a distinct similarity in design between this mosaic adjacent to the ambulatory and the mosaics at Yarchester in Shropshire and Verulamium XXVII.3

Illustration PSANHS XCVII (1952) pl X i

LULLINGSTONE, Kent

TQ 5365   4th cent   f 1949   On view in situ (Site Museum)

An older country house, which had fallen into disuse, was taken over and modernised, mosaic floors being laid in the 4th century. Later still the bath block was converted into a room for Christian worship, the walls being painted with Chi-Rhos and robed figures with their arms outstretched in prayer. A large apsed room has a mosaic pavement into which has been crammed an assortment of figured and geometric designs. The main rectangle is bordered on three sides by an unusual double swastika pattern. Within this a square holds a large guilloche cushion-shape with Bellerophon killing a small and harmless-looking Chimaera, while four dolphins cavort uncomfortably in the corners. Circles in the four corners of the square hold robed busts of the Seasons, Winter being heavily hooded and Spring having a swallow perched on her shoulder. On the sides small crosses and triangles probably flanked an urn. Between this square and the apse is a rectangle with a jumble of geometric designs, such as crosses, swastikas, hearts, chequers, duplex knots and so on. A small step leads up to the apse, where a horseshoe-shaped panel is bordered by a double looped ribbon, a superior version of one found at Worplesdon in Surrey. Here is depicted in simple outline the rape of Europa, who is sitting nonchalantly on the back of Zeus, in the guise of a lively white bull bounding across the sea, accompanied by two large Cupids. An inscription in Latin reads 'invida si ta[uri] vidisset Iuno natatus iustius Aeolias isset adusque domos' (If Juno in her jealousy had seen the bull swimming thus, she might with greater justice have gone to the halls of Aeolus). At Keynsham in Somerset there is a scene showing Europa sitting on the bull before their departure for Crete.

Illustrations Toynbee (1963) pls 228-229 & Meates (1955) pls 3-9

LYDNEY, Glos
SO 6102   4th cen.   Covered over in situ

Excavations in 1805 and 1928 revealed a temple, built in circa AD 367 and dedicated to the Celtic god of healing Nodens, a bath block, a guest house and a long narrow building, all lying within the confines of a protective wall. The sick probably came here to seek healing and among the various votive offerings, found in and around the temple, were numerous effigies of dogs, offerings to Nodens in his guise as a hunting god. A number of mosaic and tessellated floors were found, although many had been destroyed.

1. The Temple
a. (The *Cella* LXIII)   Lost
   A funnel running through the mosaic bedding into the ground was set in a frieze with a Latin inscription, which is thought to read as follows;
   D[eo] N[odenti] T[itus] Fl[a]vius Senilis, pr[aepositus] rel[iquationi], ex stipibus possuit o[pus cur]ante Victorino inter[pret]e. (To the god Nodens, Titus Flavius Senilis, officer in charge of the supply depot of the fleet, laid this pavement out of money offerings, the work being in charge of Victorinus, interpreter on the Governor's staff.) A second frieze has fish and dolphins swimming in all directions, two of the dolphins having

on the tips of their tails the heads of animals looking at each other in some surprise. The third frieze has a series of guilloche bordered circles, with fish swimming between them.

Illustration Wheeler (1932) pl XIXa   Reference Toynbee (1964) 271

b. (Room LXIV)

In one of the side chapels is a rectangle of chequers and a square enclosing an unusual wreath of ivy leaf scroll, similar to that at Wadfield in Gloucestershire, with a duplex knot in the centre and small chequers in the spandrels.

Illustration Wheeler (1932) pl XIXb

c. (Room LXV)

An all-over pattern of peltae.

Illustration Wheeler (1932) pl XXIIa

2. The Guest House

a. (Room XIV)

A striking 'rug' of guilloche mat.

Illustration Wheeler (1932) pl XXIIb

b. (Room XVIII)

A large circle, within a square, holds two interlaced guilloche squares framing a stylised flower in a medallion, and flower buds and tendrils fill the spandrels. A panel on one side of the mosaic has a scroll of guilloche bordered circles framing minute chequers.

Illustration Wheeler (1932) pl XXb

c. (Corridor XI)

Two adjacent rectangular panels, one with two coloured squares and triangles running diagonally across the panel, and the other with all-over peltae pattern.

Illustration Wheeler (1932) pl XXa

3. Bath Block

a. (Room XLI)   In porch of Lydney Park House

A narrow semi-circular guilloche bordered panel framing a fluted urn.

Illustration Wheeler (1932) pl XIXc

b. (Room XXXV)

A fragment of peltae pattern

Illustration Wheeler (1932) pl I

4. The Long Building

a. (Room L)

A heavy guilloche bordered square holds interlaced guilloche squares framing a stylised flower with ivy leaf petals in a central medallion. The spandrels and one narrow panel are filled with small chequers.

Illustration Wheeler (1932) pl XXI

b. (Room LI)

A fragment of a guilloche braided panel and a medallion with chequered spandrels.
Illustration Wheeler (1932) pl XIXc

MALTON *(Derventio)*, Yorks
SE 7971   4th cent   f 1949   In Roman Malton Museum

Soon after the fort was built, a civilian town grew up on the site. An attractive but badly damaged mosaic, found in a large house, has interlaced guilloche squares overlapping the geometric borders of the surrounding square. Of the two flanking rectangular panels, all that survives is a muffled bust of Winter holding a bare twig and a semi-circle framing a long-eared dog wearing a collar. There is an outer border of chequers.
Illustration YAJ XLI (1963-6) pl IX

MANSFIELD WOODHOUSE, Notts
SK 5264   4th cent (?)   f 1786

A small and simple villa had a tessellated corridor and two rooms with mosaics, one of which was destroyed. The other had an uninspired arrangement of perspective boxes, forming stars, and framing a central medallion.
Illustration Smith, D J (1969) pl 3.23

MEDBOURNE, Leics
SP 7992   4th cent (?)   Lost   plate 10A

First found in 1721 and re-excavated several times until, in 1877, it was finally destroyed. A very striking geometric mosaic with pelta-duplex-swastika borders on two sides, and on the third an apse with a simple grid. One half of the floor has an all-over pattern of perspective boxes forming nine stars and enclosing panels of guilloche squares, meander pattern, duplex knots and so on. The second half is unique, having an elongated saltire with an oval centre and the arms decorated with four-petalled flowers and little leaves. Semi-circles between the arms of the cross have an unusual scale pattern, whilst the remaining panels frame leafy twigs.
Illustration VCH Leicestershire I (1907) pl VIIa

MOULTON, Northants
SP 7864   f 1938   Fragment in Central Museum, Northampton

A very small fragment, said to have been part of a border of conventional leaf pattern.
Reference VCH Northamptonshire I (1902) 194

NETHER HEYFORD, Northants

SP 6658   4th cent (?)   f 1699   Lost

An all-over pattern of perspective boxes framing panels of duplex knots, guilloche and lotus flowers.

Illustration VCH Northamptonshire I (1902) fig 24

NEWPORT (Shide), IOW

SZ 5088   2nd cent (?)   f 1926   On view in situ (Site Museum

This appears to be a small corridor villa with a large bath suite and several simple mosaic and tessellated floors.

a. (Room I)

A fragmentary mosaic with borders of chequers and guilloche.

b. (Room V)

A broad border of white tesserae round a square of red and white chequers.

c. (Room VI)

A long narrow room has a border of guilloche, apparently enclosing a plain central panel.

Illustration Ant J IX (1929) pl XIII

NEWTON ST LOE, Somerset

ST 7165   4th cent (?)   f 1837   plate 2B

A villa found during the construction of the Great Western Railway from Bath to Bristol, had a long corridor and a number of rooms with mosaic pavements. The only illustration of most of these mosaics is a plan in the Haverfield Collection in the Ashmolean Museum, Oxford.

a. (Room 1)

Part of the corridor has one rectangular panel of large black and white chequers framing a perspective box star and another panel has smaller chequers.

b. (Room 2)

An all-over swastika pattern in black on white enclosing two small panels of red and a central square with a pelta-duplex-swastika; there is one border of lozenges.

c. (Room 3)   Fragments stored in Bristol City Museum

In a central medallion Orpheus is seated playing his lyre to a dog-like fox, while a variety of wild beasts leap among trees in the surrounding circular frieze. On one side is a panel of pelta-duplex-swastikas and on the other a panel divided into four squares, filled respectively with four small swastikas, small interlaced circles, a pelta-duplex-swastika and a lozenge star. The whole mosaic has a border of concentric lozenges in simple outline. This, the principal room, is divided from the next by two short walls, having on the threshold an effective acanthus leaf scroll with a central medallion framing the head of a woman wearing a diadem.

11 Durngate Street, Dorchester. Geometric with urns and serpents

12A (*above*) Dyer Street, Cirencester. Mythological figures and The Seasons. (From *Illustrations of the Remains of Ancient Art in Cirencester*, 1850); photograph RCHM)
12B (below) Newton St Loe, Somerset. Plan of villa with mosaics. (From coloured lithograph by Thomas Jones)

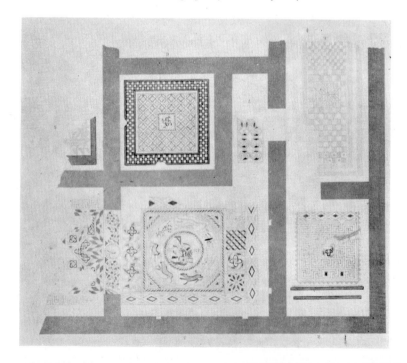

Illustrations Smith, D J (1969) pl 3.10 & JRS XXVI (1936) fig 5

d. (Room 4)

The mosaic in this adjoining room was fragmentary, but appeared to have perspective boxes decorated with red and white lozenges forming a central star and framing panels of duplex knots and guilloche 'L' shapes; there are two borders of swastikas.

e. (Room 5)

A corner of a very fragmentary mosaic shows one border of two-coloured bisected squares, stepped triangles and part of an urn.

f. (Room 6)   Panel in Bristol City Museum

Interlaced circles surround a central square framing a pelta-duplex-swastika, the whole bordered by red and white chequers.

g. (Room 7)

A small corridor room has strange circles, apparently formed by pairs of heavy peltae, some overlapping the others.

No published illustrations.

NORTH LEIGH, Oxon

SP 3915   f circa 1814

Starting as a small building in the 1st century, this villa was enlarged and re-built several times to enclose three sides of a courtyard. Most of the floors, laid in the 4th century, are very interesting in that they have much in common with mosaics found as far apart as Gloucestershire, Hampshire, Hertfordshire and Sussex.

a. (Room 1)   On view in situ (Site Museum)

An attractive rectangular mosaic has a row of three saltires, the arms all decorated with lozenges and pelta urns with convolutes. The central medallions frame stylised flowers or duplex knots, and between the arms of the crosses are two square guilloche mats. At one end a panel of a strange guilloche meander pattern leads to an adjacent square recess with another saltire, the short arms composed of decorated lozenges, and the central square framing a duplex knot surrounded by four peltae with tendrils.

Illustrations Ant J XLIX (1969) pls XL and XLII & Hakewill (1826) pl 2 fig 1

b. (Room 8)

A large circle in a square holds interlaced guilloche squares set round a medallion framing a stylised flower, composed of a central duplex knot with lotus bud and ivy leaf petals; the spandrels may have contained stylised flowers and triangular guilloche mats.

Illustration Hakewill (1826) pl 2 fig 2

c. (Room 9)

A badly damaged mosaic has four pairs of interlaced guilloche squares, two (?) of which each held a medallion with a stylised flower, and two (?)

125

held smaller interlaced squares, framing a smaller medallion. The contents of the central octagon and of four semi-circles on the sides were destroyed. Although the design of this pavement is similar to those found in The Avenue, Cirencester and Room 56 at Bignor, Sussex, it also resembles one at Bramdean, Hampshire, which has four pairs of interlaced squares.
Illustration Hakewill (1826) pl 3 fig 2

d. (Room 10)
A fragmentary mosaic 'composed of interesting circles'.
Reference Morgan (1886) 118

e. (Room 24)
A rectangular room with an apse has heavy borders of guilloche and framed in the apse is a simple scallop shell. The main part of the room is composed of a square of all-over swastika pattern, framing small squares and a central guilloche mat surrounded by four little twists of guilloche, and is flanked by two panels with pelta-duplex-swastikas alternating with badly executed plain swastikas.
Illustration Hakewill (1826) pl 3 fig 1

f. (Room 30)   2nd cent
A large saltire with borders of guilloche and wave crests, the central medallion destroyed, has each arm of the cross decorated with a tall fluted urn topped by a stylised flower, and semi-circles round the sides hold segmented stylised flowers. There is one narrow outer panel of ivy leaf and lotus flower ribbon scroll. The general design, the decoration of the tall urns and the heavy borders are all very similar to the lion mosaic in XXI.2.4 at Verulamium.
Illustration Hakewill (1826) pl 3 fig 3

NORTON DISNEY, Lincs
SK 8560   f 1937   Fragments in Newark on Trent Museum

An 'L' shaped villa, surrounded by defensive ditches, had at least two mosaic pavements.
a. A fragment of perspective box pattern, decorated with ivy leaves, peltae and stippling, frames five square panels, one with a pelta-duplex-swastika. This mosaic is somewhat similar to one of the pavements found at Denton.
b. Fragments of an all-over swastika pattern framing five squares, each containing a duplex knot.
Illustration Ant J XVII (1937) fig 9

NUNNEY (Whatley), Somerset
ST 7447   3rd cent (?)   f 1837   Lost

Although this was probably a large villa with a number of sophisticated mosaic floors, only two adjacent mosaics have been recorded as a result of several excavations; these were still on view in situ in 1906, but have since been almost totally destroyed.

a. A rectangular apsed pavement has a dolphin in a semi-circle, from which radiate four panels with urns and sprays of leaves. A panel of diagonal chequers leads to a very badly damaged square, with a panel of large chequers on the other side. The central panel of the square probably held the figure of Orpheus, but only a flower in one corner survived, and it is surrounded by a frieze of wild animals interspersed with unusual trees.

b. plate 15A
A broad rectangular panel of peltae pattern links this mosaic to the side of the last and at the far end an oblong panel frames several fishes and two (?) sea-beasts facing each other. A roundel, within a rectangle, holds a female wearing a mural crown and, in one version, holding a cornucopia and, in the other version, two corn ears; a pair of dolphins play above and below the medallion. A graceful scroll border is composed of acanthus leaves and fruit flowing from cornucopiae.
Illustration Coloured drawing in Somerset County Museum, Taunton & VCH Somerset I (1906) fig 77 Ref PSANHS 114 (1970) 37

OLDCOATES, Notts
SK 5988 f 1870 Covered over in situ (?)

A mosaic was found after the digging of foundations for a church and described at the time by the architect: 'Close to the south end on the west side was the entrance, marked by a step down and a threshold; at this end . . . the pattern of the floor being a chequer of 12 in. squares, red and grey alternately . . . 7 feet in width; to this succeeds a band, 14 inches wide, of smaller tesserae, arranged in a very graceful design of scrolls and squares. The centre portion of this band is imperfect, and was not a mere repetition of the design . . . The remainder of the design consists of a labyrinth almost identical with that discovered at Caerleon . . . The labyrinth, 9 feet 6 inches square . . . is surrounded by a border of triangles, alternately red and grey . . . The centre of the labyrinth, 2 feet 7 inches square, was unfortunately much injured, but the lower portion of a human figure remained, in an attitude of attack; one arm had been extended, with a short broad sword pointed downwards, the lower part of the blade remaining; and over the shoulder the outline of an oval shield was evident. The tesserae were very small . . . ' This figure is presumed to be Theseus in the Cretan labyrinth.
Reference Arch J XXVIII (1871) 66

OULSTON, Yorks
SE 5674 f before 1857 In the Yorkshire Museum, York

a. A long narrow room or corridor was divided into three square panels. The first holding a large circle of guilloche, which flows into the centre to form four small medallions and a larger central circle framing the bust of a wide-eyed female; between the medallions and in the spandrels are clumsy heart-shapes with tendrils. Next, a square panel of guilloche mat leads to another panel with a border of cramped swastika pattern enclosing four swastikas and five squares with guilloche mat, pelta-duplex-swastikas and, in the centre, a star formed of perspective boxes.

b. A raised apse is again bordered by cramped swastika pattern framing a colourful urn with two bare trees growing from the base.

Reference The Yorkshire Museum Handbook (1891) 93

PITMEADS (Sutton Veny), Wilts
ST 9043   f 1785   Lost

Fragments of several mosaic pavements found between 1785 and 1800 were all destroyed after drawings had been made, apart from one piece which was taken to Longleat but cannot now be traced.

a. f 1785
A small medallion, bordered with guilloche or twisted ribbon, framing a strange stylised flower.
Illustration Hoare (1819) fig 1

b. f 1786
A long narrow panel or corridor with a central strip of small double twists of ribbon (?) bordered by guilloche.
Illustration Hoare (1819) fig 2

c. f 1786
A large fragment shows guilloche and swastika pattern bordering three panels, the contents of one being totally destroyed. The next is narrow and holds a hare crouching among curious forms, possibly intended as rocks; a hare among leafy plants was found in Beeches Road, Cirencester in 1971. The third panel has a heavily robed figure with the head destroyed, but reminiscent of the Muses (?) at Aldborough in Yorkshire.
Illustration Hoare (1819) fig 3

d. f 1800
Small chequers surround a guilloche bordered square enclosing a large guilloche medallion with most of the contents destroyed. It has been suggested that the tiny fragments which survived show the legs of an animal, indicating that this is an Orpheus mosaic, but on this evidence alone I do not think that such an assumption is justified. In the spandrels are stylised leaf sprays.
Illustration Hoare (1819) fig 4

PITNEY, Somerset
4th cent

1. ST 4530   f 1828   Lost
A courtyard villa with several mosaic and tessellated floors.

a. Two rooms divided by short walls, both have fine mosaics; in the smaller
    room it runs right over the threshold and is composed of five large guilloche
    swastikas framing four panels with cupids in the guise of the Seasons,
    Spring holding a sickle and flowers, Summer a striped cannister and a bird,
    and Autumn a rake, Winter having been destroyed. The larger room has a
    central octagon containing Bacchus, from which radiate eight flat-topped
    triangles framing alternately male and female figures, including Neptune,
    Mercury (?) and Orpheus (?). In the four corners are busts, presumably of
    Wind gods, since three of them hold a conch shell, but the fourth has only
    a spindly leaf.
    Illustration Smith, D J (1969) pl 3.3

b. An effective border of dark and light triangles frames a medallion, within a
    square, holding a naked man, possibly Cadmus upsetting his bucket of
    water as he strikes at the serpent guarding the spring.
    Illustration VCH Somerset I (1906) fig 86

c. A rectangular panel with an all-over pattern of interlaced circles enclosing
    small squares.
    Illustration VCH Somerset I (1906) fig 85

2. ST 4429   exc 1861
Lying to the south of the other and better known Pitney villa is a site which
was first detected in 1828, but not excavated until 1861 and then only
partially explored and sparsely recorded. A very simple mosaic was found
showing a rectangle with two guilloche squares, each holding a plain circle
framing two plain squares, not interlaced, with a stylised flower in one and
concentric circles in the other
*Illustration Drawing in Somerset County Museum, Taunton   Reference VCH
Somerset I (1906) 328*

PONTESBURY see LEA CROSS

PRESTON (Weymouth), Dorset
SY 7082   f 1852   Covered over in situ (?)

In addition to several tessellated floors, one simple geometric mosaic was
found and left open under a hut for nearly 100 years, during which time it
suffered much damage and was finally covered over with concrete. The
mosaic is rectangular with two panels of simple ivy leaf scroll flanking a
square, which is cut by guilloche to form a large octagon. A central guilloche

129

bordered square frames a stylised flower and the remaining spaces within the octagon are filled with triangles and oblong panels, each holding a small piece of meander pattern.

Illustration RCHM Dorset II.3 (1970) pl 225

RAMPISHAM, Dorset
ST 5503   f 1799   Lost

According to Hutchins' *History of Dorset,* a large mosaic pavement was found and 'from its situation in the midst of an uncultivated common, west of the vill (sic), the largeness of the dies, nearly two inches square, and there being no vestiges of any building, it seems to have formed the floor of an officer's tent.' A drawing shows an unusual design, with a large twelve-petalled flower in the centre and concentric quarter-circles in each corner. This interpretation of the mosaic may be as inaccurate as the suggestion that it was the floor of a tent, but some plain tesserae were found on the site in the 1930s.

Illustration Hutchins 3rd ed II (1863) 692

RAPSLEY (Ewhurst), Surrey
TQ 0841   3rd cent   f 1965

In the early years of the 3rd century an aisled house and a separate bath block were built, with one mosaic and several tessellated floors. Later this bath building was converted into a small dwelling house and another mosaic was laid in an extension.

a. (Room 4)

A long room with a mosaic, similar in style to one found at North Hill in Colchester, Essex, has a central square panel, the contents lost, a guilloche octagon framing a stylised flower on each side, and near each corner a guilloche 'L' shape, the background being filled with simple perspective boxes.

Illustration SyAC LXV (1968) pl VII

b. (Room 9)

A simple grid in fine tesserae, unusual only in so far as the tesserae of the grid lines were missing and the spaces were said to have been filled in with mud, but they may have been removed for re-use elsewhere.

Illustration SyAC LXV (1968) pl IIb

ROCKBOURNE, Hants
SU 1217   4th cent   f 1942   On view in situ (Site Museum)

A long villa in which about sixty rooms and a number of mosaic and tessellated pavements have so far been discovered.

a. (Room I)

A corridor, cut into by an octagonal room, has a medallion, containing a star with a central duplex knot, which is flanked by panels of swastika pattern and interlaced circles.

Illustration Morley Hewitt (1969) pl III

b. (Room VIII)

Broad bands of coarse red and white tesserae surround a square panel formed of four swastikas, in smaller tesserae, framing a little stylised flower, executed in even smaller tesserae. The borders of broad bands are reminiscent of those in the labyrinth mosaic at Harpham in Yorkshire.

Illustration Morley Hewitt (1969) pl IV

c. (Room XXXIII)

A fragment shows a wide border of guilloche mat with part of an urn (?) in the corner.

Illustration Morley Hewitt (1969) pl Va

ROXBY, Lincs

SE 9216   4th cent (?)   f 1699   Covered over in situ

A striking mosaic with a border of pelta-duplex-swastikas and an all-over pattern of perspective boxes, decorated with a variety of little flowers, and possibly vine leaves, enclosing four squares of guilloche mat. In the centre is a diamond framing a stylised flower with four heart-shaped petals. There are two slightly differing versions of this mosaic, a fragment being wrongly included in drawings of Winterton.

Illustrations Fowler (1796-1818) nos 1.IV and 3 & Smith, D J (1969) pl 3.17

RUDGE FARM (Froxfield), Wilts

SU 2769   f 1725

A guilloche bordered medallion within a square was much damaged, but a drawing shows the lower portions of a female, heavily clothed, and of a man with a sword or stave; on the ground behind him, water pours from an overturned pail. It is interesting to compare this pavement with the Pitney mosaic where Cadmus (?) strikes at a serpent.

Illustration Hoare (1819) facing 121

RUDSTON, Yorks

TA 0866   4th cent   f 1933   In the Archaeology Museum, Hull

A small villa, which had a relatively short life, contained three interesting mosaic pavements.

a. This crude but amusing mosaic has childishly drawn animals and absurdly

131

posturing humans, with long bodies and arms and disproportionately short legs. A square holds a large saltire with a central medallion framing a long-haired Venus, an apple in one hand and a mirror dropping from the other; very different from the gracious Venus at Low Ham. An attendant Triton appears to be offering her a back-scratcher. Decorating the arms of the cross are naked men, armed with various weapons, hunting the lion (Leo), stag, leopard and wild bull (Taurus) which occupy semi-circles between the arms of the cross. In each corner is a bird with fruit. Of two flanking panels only one survives, showing Mercury, leaves instead of wings in his cap, and pots of leaves on either side.
Illustration Richmond (1963) pl 1
b. A fragment of an attractive pavement has a scatter of fishes, dolphins and shellfish, and among them lobster claws in the head of Neptune (?). A wreath of lotus flowers forms an attractive border and two end panels have trees and a bird, which looks very startled by an unidentifiable object.
Illustration Richmond (1963) pl 3
c. A simple but effective geometric design of four pelta-duplex-swastikas surrounded by a border of swastika pattern.
Illustration Richmond (1963) pl 2

ST ALBANS *(Verulamium)*, **Herts**
TL 1307

After the Roman invasion of AD 43, a native settlement near the present town of St Albans was granted the status of *municipium*. It was destroyed during the Boudiccan rebellion of AD 60-1 and rebuilt with a theatre, civic buildings, temples and many houses, often large, extending over an area of 200 acres. Most of the excavations on this site, which took place during the 1930s and 1950s, revealed houses with numerous mosaics and tessellated floors belonging to two main periods of construction. A number of these mosaics are well displayed in the Verulamium Museum at St Albans.
1. Insula II Building I   2nd cent   In Verulamium Museum
A well preserved apse mosaic has a border of wave crests framing a large fan-shaped scallop shell, set against a red ground.
Illustrations Wheeler (1936) pls XXXIX and XCVIIIa
2. Insula III Building II   circa AD 300
a. (Room 24)
A fragment of meander pattern border in white on black.
Illustration Wheeler (1936) pl XLIIIa and b and pl XXX (plan)
b. (Room 25)
A grid pattern could be indicated by the fragment with peltae and a duplex knot, which was all that survived.

Illustrations Wheeler (1936) pl XLIVa and pl XXX (plan)

3. **Insula IV** Building I (Room 5)   2nd cent   In Verulamium Museum

A grid pattern with squares and rectangles superimposed on a large circle with borders of wave crests, guilloche and uneven stepped triangles. A large 'dahlia' occupies the central square, together with two tiny lotus flowers and two convoluted ivy leaves, and in each corner square is a smaller stylised flower. There are two narrow borders of diamonds. This mosaic is so like pavements found at Colchester, in Essex, that I feel they must have come either from the same pattern book or from the hand of the same mosaicist.

Illustrations Wheeler (1936) pl XLIVb and XXXI (plan)

4. **Insula IV** Building II (Room 29)   2nd cent   Part in City Hall, St Albans and part in Verulamium Museum

A very striking pavement is divided in two by a panel of floral scroll; the smaller part of the floor has a border of wave crests framing perspective boxes forming four stars and decorated with guilloche, lotus buds and stippling. The larger part of the floor has a border of swastikas and on one side a narrow panel of lotus bud and ivy leaf scroll. Perspective boxes decorated with various devices, including hearts, ivy leaves, guilloche and diamonds, frame five medallions with stylised flowers and borders of wave crests and stepped triangles.

Illustrations Wheeler (1936) pls XL and XLVIa and pl XXXI (plan)

5. **Insula IV** Building VIII

a. (Room 4)   2nd cent   In Verulamium Museum

A central square holds the bust of a bearded and muscular Neptune, lobster claws sprouting from his head. A wide border of swastikas encloses panels framing four large stylised flowers and four small, but well proportioned, urns, two of which appear to hold a ladle.

Illustrations Wheeler (1936) pls XLI and XLVa and pl XXXII (plan)

b. (Room 6)

i. 2nd cent

A fragment of brightly coloured perspective boxes and guilloche was found in the hypocaust.

Illustration Wheeler (1936) pl XLVIIIa

ii. circa AD 300   On view in situ in Verulamium Park

A panel of uninspired acanthus leaf scroll is all that remains of a large pavement.

Illustration Wheeler (1936) pl XLII

c. (Room 7)   2nd cent   On view in situ in Verulamium Park

A large grid of sixteen guilloche squares, each framing a medallion with a large stylised flower, of which there are eight different types. On two sides are panels of quatrefoils formed by shaded interlaced circles.

Illustrations Wheeler (1936) pls XLII and XLVb and pl XXXII (plan)

133

d. (Room 15)   circa AD 300   In Verulamium Museum
A fragment of a mosaic panel with an all-over pattern of pelta-duplex-swastikas.
Illustration Wheeler (1936) pl XLVIb and XXXII (plan)

6. Insula IV Building X

a. (Room 9)   2nd cent
Fragments of mosaic, found in the hypocaust, formed a border of swastika pattern enclosing floral and guilloche panels round a central urn flanked by lively dolphins. There is no illustrated record of the borders.
Illustration Wheeler (1936) pl XLVII

b. (Corridor)   circa AD 300   Covered over in situ
At one end of the corridor is a square panel of black and white chequers and scattered 'L' shapes, somewhat reminiscent of the mosaic in the church (?) at Silchester.
Illustration Wheeler (1936) pl XLVIIIb

7. Insula XIV Building 5

a. (Room 3)   4th cent   In Verulamium Museum
An interesting fragment with a lion attacking a deer.
Illustration Ant J XXXIX (1959) fig 4 (plan)

b. (Room 5)   circa AD 300
A fragment of perspective box pattern with small panels of guilloche.
Illustration Ant J XXXIX (1959) fig 4 (plan)

8. Insula XXI Building II (Room 4)   2nd cent (?)   In Verulamium Museum
A heavy saltire within a square has a large central panel containing a lion stalking off with the bloody head of a stag in his jaws. Four well-proportioned urns decorate the arms of the cross, and stylised flowers fill the intervening semi-circles.
Illustration Ant J XL (1960) pls I and IIIb

9. Insula XXVII Building II   Late 4th cent

a. (Room 3)   In Verulamium Museum
Fragments of mosaic show a border of swastikas with a large stylised flower in a central guilloche medallion, and sprays of ivy leaves in the spandrels. It is interesting to compare this with two other very similar mosaics found at Yarchester in Shropshire and Lufton in Somerset.
Illustration Ant J XXXVIII (1958) pl IIIa

b. (Room 8)   Fragments in Verulamium Museum
Small fragments show that this mosaic must have been composed of an all-over swastika pattern framing numerous squares containing stylised flowers, peltae, guilloche mats and an urn. A centrally placed head wearing a wreath was possibly Bacchus. A fragment of an adjacent panel with perspective box pattern is thought to be of an earlier date.
Illustration Ant J XL (1960) pl V

10. Insula XXVIII Building III   2nd cent   In Verulamium Museum

A grid pattern with squares and rectangles, very similar to the mosaic found at Ashcroft Road in Cirencester, has in the centre a large urn from which rise two jets of water and there are two dolphins with tails wound round each handle. The remaining panels are filled with guilloche diamonds, chequers and an arrangement which could be a stylised flower.

Illustration Ant J XXXIX (1959) pl IVa

SAPCOTE, Leics
SP 4993   f 1770   Lost

'A curious tessellated pavement nearly similar to that found some years ago near the Cathedral at Lincoln.' This account presumably refers to the mosaic found in the Cathedral cloisters, so that the design would have included the perspective box pattern and perhaps another linked hearts and lotus flowers motif.

Reference Nichols, J History and Antiquities of the County of Leicester IV (1811) 898

SCAMPTON, Lincs
SK 9578   4th cent (?)   f 1795   Lost

The villa found here had thirteen fragmentary pavements, many of them said to have been coarse, and one fine corridor mosaic with a border of interlaced circles. Rectangular and square panels contain a riot of the usual geometric patterns, including perspective boxes, peltae, pelta-duplex-swastikas and duplex knots. The most interesting panel has four guilloche medallions and four 'L' shapes round a square with a central guilloche cross and four small duplex knots between the arms.

Illustration Smith, D J (1969) pl 3.22

SEATON, Devon
SY 2390   4th cent (?)   f 1920

A complex of buildings covering at least 12 acres may be a large villa estate. So far only one mosaic has been found, in an unpretentious residential block, showing a crudely drawn lotus flower in a corner panel bordered with guilloche.

Illustration TDA LIV (1923) facing 68

SEAVINGTON, Somerset
ST 4013   f 1861

It was reported in a local newspaper that a villa had been found with at least

135

one large room and a passage paved with a mosaic in large chequers.
Reference Gents Mag 1862 i 298

SHIDE see NEWPORT

SILCHESTER *(Calleva A trebatum)*, **Hants**
SU 6462

This *civitas* capital now lies beneath agricultural land within the ruins of its
fortifications. Excavations occurred circa 1740-50 and 1833 and the area was
systematically explored in 1864-78 and 1890-1909, when a plan of the town
was established; subsequent work having added some chronological details.
There was a regular grid of streets forming some forty *insulae*, which contained numerous houses, mostly widely spaced, those in alignment with the
streets being usually of 2nd or 3rd century dating. The majority of the pavements are plain or simple geometric design, but unfortunately many have
been destroyed by ploughing. Although the illustrations of most of the mosaics
may be found in copies of the *Archaeologia,* to which I have given references
here, a more precise report of the excavations may be found in G. C. Boon's
Roman Silchester (1957)
1. **Insula I** Building I   In Stratfield Saye House
a. A dominating central medallion framing a large urn is set among perspective boxes decorated with duplex knots, guilloche twists and peltae.
Illustration Arch XLVI (1881) pl XIII
b. Small fragments of a border of foliate scroll and ivy leaves.
*Illustrations Joyce, J G 'Journal of Excavations at Silchester' ms in
Reading Museum & Arch XLVI (1881) pl XI (plan)*
2. **Insula I** Building 2
a. (North Corridor)
A simple and unusual pattern composeα of plain red borders and a central
stripe in red on white, with a plain red and black octagon superimposed on
the stripe at the western end of the corridor, and a red and black hexagon
in the same position at the eastern end, possibly the layout for some game.
Illustrations Arch LII (1890) pls XXVIII and XXIX
b. (West Corridor)
A swastika pattern enclosing small panels of guilloche.
Illustration Arch LII (1890) pl XXVIII (plan)
c. (Room 2)   4th cent (?)
A fragmentary border of rainbow pattern which, used in this way, is quite
unique in Britain.
*Illustrations Fox Collection Box 5.13 in Soc of Ant of London & Arch
LII (1890) pl XXVIII (plan)*

3. Insula II Building 1

a. (Room 9)   Stored in Reading Museum

A small square panel set to one side of the room frames a bold stylised flower executed in red and white.

Illustrations Fox Collection Box 5.15 in Soc of Ant of London & Arch LIII (1892) pl XXII (plan)

b. (Room 10)

A much damaged square panel contains a diamond framing a stylised flower with ivy leaf petals and in each outer corner a lotus urn.

Illustrations Fox Collection Box 5.14 in Soc of Ant of London & Arch LIII (1892) pl XXII (plan)

4. Insula II Building 2 (Room 11)

Fragments of a border of red and white chequers was all that survived of a patterned mosaic.

Illustration Arch LIII (1892) pl XXIII

5. Insula IV Church (?)   4th cent   In Reading Museum

A building lying near the south-east corner of the forum, appears to have been a small church. In front of the apse there is a simple and attractive mosaic with a central square of black and white chequers and 'L' shapes, bordered by large red and grey diamonds.

Illustrations Arch LIII (1893) pl XL & Boon (1957) pl 8

6. Insula VI Building 2 (Room 4)

A house with a number of tessellated floors had a small room with a simple and coarsely executed pattern of interlaced rectangles in alternate red and fawn tesserae, with bordering stripes.

Reference Arch LX (1906) 159

7. Insula VIII Building 1

a. (Room 6)

A square mosaic, much damaged, was divided by guilloche into four panels, apparently all framing stylised flowers and ivy leaves.

Illustration Arch LIV (1894) pl XVIII (plan)

b. (Room 9)

A plain drab tessellated floor has a broad band of black along one side of the room and, on the opposite side, an even broader band of red and black.

Illustrations Fox Collection Box 5.34 in Soc of Ant of London & Arch LIV (1894) pl XVIII (plan)

8. Insula XIV Building 1

a. (Room 22)   Two fragments in Reading Museum

Perspective boxes, decorated with pelta-duplex-swastikas, ivy leaves and guilloche, frame five guilloche medallions, each with a stylised flower.

Illustration Arch LV (1896) pl XII

b. (Room 23)   In Reading Museum

A striking all-over pattern of swastikas framing small square panels, with a variety of geometric designs, including triangles, rectangles, chequers, 'T' and 'L' shapes, all in black on a white ground. Although the decorations are less sophisticated, this mosaic is very similar to one of the late 4th century in Insula XXVII.2.8 at Verulamium.
Illustration Arch LV (1896) pl XIII

c. (Room 24)
Only small fragments remained of a grid of sixteen guilloche bordered octagons.
Illustration Arch LV (1896) pl XI (plan)

d. (Room 27)   In Reading Museum
A unique grid of nine hexagons, with borders of floral and foliate scroll, wave crests, lotus buds in pairs and ivy leaves, each framing a stylised flower; with the exception of the central hexagon which holds an urn. The intervening spaces are filled with lozenge swastikas.
Illustration Arch LV (1896) pl XIV

9. Insula XIV Building 2   Fragments stored in Reading Museum

a. (Room 12)
A small square of perspective boxes encloses four guilloche 'L' shapes round a central diamond with contents destroyed.
Illustrations Fox Collection Box 5.9 in Soc of Ant of London & Arch LV (1896) pl XV (plan)

b. (Gallery 14)
This 54 ft long gallery has a mosaic divided into a series of square and rectangular panels, several of which had been destroyed, but at least one held a bust. There is a wide border of chequers and swastikas.
i. Coarse red and white stripes
ii. Two guilloche bordered squares framing stylised flowers.
iii. The bust of a female wearing a mural crown (?)
iv. A central medallion flanked by baskets of fruit (?) in which blue glass tesserae appeared.
v. A large and badly damaged square, with a central medallion and small circles in the corners, is flanked by rectangular panels of guilloche mat.
Illustrations Fox Collection Box 5.7 in Soc of Ant London & Arch LV (1896) pl XV (plan)

c. (Room 20)
Stripes and concentric rectangles in red and white are bordered by a broad red band.
Illustrations Fox Collection Box 5.10 in Soc of Ant of London & Arch LV (1896) pl XV (plan)

10. Insula XIX Building 2 (Room A)   Fragments in Reading Museum
This was thought to be a very early mosaic, but the surviving fragments

suggest a grid pattern design similar to the 2nd century mosaics at Colchester and Verulamium. In one of the rectangles the hindquarters of an animal and some tendrils can be seen, indicating that there was probably an urn flanked by two beasts, as at Littlecote in Wiltshire. Two of the squares hold the remains of heads, certainly in the one case of an unusual profile type. One surviving border has a delicate floral scroll springing from a central pedestal, on which stands a small winged Cupid; another has the leaves of two trees and a fragment of a red cloak (?), thought to be part of a hunting scene; and a third border has a ribbon scroll framing simple cruciform flowers. Along one side is a large panel with a flowing spray of smilax worked in black on a white ground.
Illustrations Arch LVI (1899) pl XIV & Boon (1957) pl 11
11. Insula XXI Building 1
A small house with red and white tessellated floors and in a rectangular recess off the corridor, a fragment of perspective box pattern.
Illustration Arch XL (1866) pl XXIII (plan)
12. Insula XXI Building 4 (Room 8)
A fragmentary mosaic shows perspective boxes, decorated with duplex knots, and eight guilloche panels set round a central guilloche bordered medallion. An ivy leaf occupies the one surviving corner.
Illustration Fox Collection Box 5.18 in Soc of Ant of London Reference Arch LVII (1900) 94
13. Insula XXIII Building 1
a. (Corridor 2)
   A roughly executed mosaic with longitudinal bands in various shades of red.
   Illustration Arch XL (1866) pl XXIV (plan)
b. (Room 3)   In Reading Museum
   An interesting floor is composed of square, octagonal and hexagonal tiles loosly fitted together like the cells of a honeycomb, the interstices being filled with tesserae.
   Illustration Arch LVII (1901) pl XXVII
14. Insula XXIII Building 2
a. (Room 14)
   Wide borders of coarse red tesserae, dentil pattern and large stepped triangles surround a square, executed in fine tesserae, with panels of duplex knots in each corner and swastika pattern round a central square panel, contents destroyed.
   Illustration Fox Collection Box 5.19 in Soc of Ant of London Reference Arch LVII (1901) 232
b. (Room 18)
   A large damaged rectangle bordered with guilloche is divided into four rectangular panels; two hold a diamond with a border of stepped.

triangles, one framing a fluted urn and the other an unusual lotus urn, the outer corners having single leaves and flowers. The third panel frames a dolphin within a border of wave crests and the fourth, and missing panel, probably had a similar design.

Illustration Arch LVII (1901) pl XXVIII

15. Insula XXVII Building 1

a. (Room 16)

A square mosaic bordered by red bands and set to one side of a large room, has a guilloche bordered saltire with a stylised flower in the central medallion and panels of duplex knot decorating the arms of the cross. Segmented flowers occupy the semi-circles between the arms and there is a single heart in each corner

Illustration Fox Collection Box 5.1 in Soc of Ant of London   Reference Arch LVIII (1902) 21

b. (Room 17)   Fragment in Reading Museum

A winter room 'had in the floor a large central panel of fine mosaic set in a red ground, [i.e. cement bedding] but with the exception of a small fragment at one corner with a bust of a figure of Flora (?), this had been entirely destroyed.' The bust, which is very crudely executed and is probably one of the Seasons, is wearing a grey garment and has red flowers, and a twig (?) over the shoulder.

References Arch LVIII (1902) 21 & Boon (1957) and 2nd ed forthcoming

c. (Room 18)   In Reading Museum

The threshold of an annexe to Room 16 has a panel of triangles with curved sides bordered by guilloche, leading to an almost circular mosaic skilfully bordered by black swastika pattern. The central panel was destroyed, apart from a fragment of wave crest border and the suggestion of a central figure.

Illustration Arch LVIII (1902) pl III

d. (Room 27)

Coarse red and white bands border a broad-armed saltire decorated with circles and with one leaf in a semi-circle between the arms of the cross. The central panel is destroyed.

Illustration Fox Collection Box 5.8 in Soc of Ant of London Reference Arch LVIII (1902) 23

16. Insula XXXIV Building 1

a. (Room 2)   In Stratfield Saye House

A large square has a guilloche saltire with a four-petalled stylised flower in the central roundel and pelta urns with spirals, ivy leaves and quartered lozenges decorating the arms. The design is very similar to one found at Tockington Park in Gloucestershire.

b. A panel of ivy leaf and lotus bud scroll.

Illustration Arch LX (1907) pl XLI

13A
(*left*) Bignor,
Sussex (Room 56).
Interlaced squares
and Medusa.
(From Samuel
Lysons, *Reliquiae
Britannico-
Romanae* III, 1817,
plate XXVIII)

13B
(*below*) The
Avenue (?),
Cirencester.
Interlaced squares.
(From Samuel
Lysons, *Reliquiae
Britannico-
Romanae* II, 1817,
plate V)

14A
(*left*) Whittlebury
Northamptonshire
Victoria (?) (From
an engraving in the
Journal of the
British
Archaeological
Association VII,
1852, plate XI)

14B
(*right*) Itchen
Abbas, Hampshire
(Room 3). Flora (?)
(From an engraving
in the Journal
of the British
Archaeological
Association
XXXIV, 1878, 504)

SLINFOLD, Sussex
TQ 1133   f circa 1912

A Roman pavement was found in 1912 but soon filled in again and left until 1934, when a piece was taken up and placed in a garden where it remained until its destruction in 1959. Large fragments were said to have been deposited in Horsham Museum, but they cannot now be traced.
Reference Sussex Notes and Queries 15.4 (1959) 132

SOUTHWELL, Notts
SK 7053   exc 1959   Covered over in situ

Close to the Minster, in the centre of Southwell, finds of mosaic and tessellated pavements have been recorded on various occasions from 1793 until 1959, when systematic excavations took place. The fragment of mosaic in the Minster, however, is not thought to be of Roman workmanship.
a. f 1901
   A considerable area of coarse mosaic with a simple grid pattern in red on a grey ground has small grey squares at the intersections.
   Reference VCH Nottinghamshire II (1910) 34
b. (Mosaic 1)   f 1959
   Another simple grid pattern, but here the grid is larger and in grey on a red ground with small red squares at the intersections.
   Illustrations Trans Thoroton Soc LXX (1966) pls 1b, 4a and fig 13
c. (Mosaic 2)   f 1959)
   A mosaic strip 'rug' composed of three square guilloche panels framing a variety of standard designs used in an unusual way. The middle panel holds a diamond, each corner resting on the back of a pelta, enclosing a stylised flower with eight ivy leaf petals, and the corners of the square holding four-petalled flowers. Each of the two flanking panels has a central duplex knot surrounded by four peltae. A duplex knot and stylised flowers probably filled the corners.
   Illustration Trans Thoroton Soc LXX (1966) pls 2, 3 and fig 11
d. (Mosaic 3)   f 1959
   A small corner fragment showed that this square mosaic had contained a large plain circle, possibly divided into five pentagonal panels, but these could have been uneven-sided hexagons with a pentagon in the centre. The spandrels have ivy leaves and tendrils and a feature of one pentagon (?) is a small panel of bisected dog's tooth triangles.
   Illustration Trans Thoroton Soc LXX (1966) fig 12
e. (Mosaic 4)   f 1959
   A fragment indicated that this had been an all-over pattern of concentric octagons interspersed with small squares in coarse grey tesserae on a red

143

ground.
Illustration Trans Thoroton Soc LXX (1966) fig 13

SPARSHOLT, Hants
SU 4130   f 1965

A villa and an aisled building, set on two sides of a courtyard, have several
rooms with mosaics, some very fragmentary.
a. (Corridor 1)
   A swastika pattern in coarse red and grey tesserae runs the length of the
   corridor.
   No published illustration   Reference JRS LVI (1966) 214
b. (Room 2)
   A floor of red and grey chequers.
   No published illustration   Reference JRS LVI (1966) 214
ç. (Room 7)   In Winchester City Museum
   A square mosaic with castellated and guilloche borders enclosing a large
   medallion, with a central eight-pointed star, bordered by guilloche, wave
   crests and swastika pattern which cleverly follow the curve of the medallion.
   Two spandrels hold portly lotus urns with tendril scroll handles and two
   have half-open fans (?), somewhat similar to the motifs in one corner of the
   mosaic found in St George's Street, Winchester.
   Illustration JRS LVII (1967) pl XV

SPAXTON, Somerset
ST 2436   4th cent   f 1964

A small courtyard type villa had three mosaic floors, all of which were so
badly damaged by ploughing that in only one could the pattern be distinguished; it has a basically black and white geometric design with a central
floral motif in red and blue-grey.
Illustration PSANHS forthcoming volume

SPOONLEY WOOD (Sudeley Manor), Glos
SP 0425   f 1882

A large villa with a number of tessellated and fine mosaic floors, much damaged by tree roots, some of which were moved or repaired with new material.
Illustration Arch LII (1890) pl XVII (plan)
a. (Room 5)
   The coarsely executed bust of a man holding a rake, probably representing
   one of the Seasons, was all that remained of this mosaic. The restored panel
   cannot now be traced at Sudeley Castle.

Illustration Winchcombe & Sudeley Record 4 (1893) fig 5
b. (Room 7)

A well disguised saltire, framed by four guilloche 'L' shapes, has a central guilloche bordered medallion holding a strange stylised flower formed of a duplex knot surrounded by 'rotating' petals. Between the arms of the cross are duplex knots in squares.

Illustration Winchcombe & Sudeley Record 4 (1893) fig 7
c. (Room 8)

A square encloses a large guilloche circle divided into seven hexagons, the one in the centre being bordered with wave crests and possibly holding a bust, while the other six frame stylised flowers. In each spandrel is a stylised floral spray.

Illustration Winchcombe & Sudeley Record 4 (1893) fig 8
d. (Room 18)

Set to one side of the room, a square mosaic, bordered with diamonds, has two interlaced guilloche squares framing a central medallion with a stylised flower. In each corner is a fluted urn, two full-bellied and broad based and two tall and thin with tendrils.

Illustration Winchcombe & Sudeley Record 4 (1893) fig 6

STANCOMBE PARK (Stinchcombe), Glos
ST 7497   f circa 1847

A number of fragments of mosaics now in Gloucester City Museum come from a private collection once kept at Stancombe Park, where a villa, with a mosaic similar to one at Woodchester, is said to have been found. Since the fragments were not labelled, it is by no means certain where they were excavated; but they are presumed to have come from Stancombe Park.
a. In Gloucester City Museum
   A corner of interlaced guilloche squares with a triangle framing a pelta urn.
b. In Gloucester City Museum
   Two borders of swastikas and duplex knots.
   Reference JBAA II (1847) 349

STONESFIELD, Oxon
SP 4017   4th cent (?)   Lost

Several mosaics were discovered in what must have been a large and richly decorated villa, the one found in 1712 being the first in Britain to be described and discussed in detail.
a. (Room B)   f 1712

A large rectangular mosaic, with a border of swastikas enclosing panels of guilloche, was divided into two squares, one of them flanked by two panels

145

of peltae pattern. One square has a border of pelta-duplex-swastikas and four swastika lozenges enclosing a large circle, which in turn frames tendril scrolls and a square of perspective boxes, decorated with guilloche 'L' shapes and duplex knots, round a small guilloche mat. In two spandrels are urns with leaves decorating the handles and in two, ivy leaves with tendrils. The second square is more ornate, having a large circle of acanthus leaf scroll springing from a bearded mask of Neptune; in the central roundel, which is bordered by meander pattern, is Bacchus wearing a wreath of vine leaves and holding his thyrsus and wine cup as he prepares to mount a fierce, but rather puny panther.

Illustration Smith, D J (1969) pl 3.15 A

b. (Room C)   f 1780

A narrow rectangle, divided into three square panels, has in the centre four plain swastikas enclosing five duplex knots, and flanking this two squares of perspective boxes.

Illustration Smith, D J (1969) pl 3.15 B

c. (Room D)   f 1780

A somewhat uninteresting square mosaic with heavy borders of guilloche, swastikas and chain pattern enclosing a square of perspective boxes.

Illustration Smith, D. J (1969) pl 3.15 C

d. (Room A)   f 1780   plate 16A

A large saltire has a central square of guilloche mat and the arms decorated with ivy leaves, lozenge swastikas and pelta ivy leaf urns, with tendril handles, set on a strikingly white ground. The triangles between the arms hold curious little lotus buds.

Illustration Soc of Ant of London Top Colls (Red Port Oxon) 39

STURTON-BY-SCAWBY, Lincs
SE 9604

a. f 1816

A rectangular mosaic with an attractive shaded scale pattern.

b. f 1817

A guilloche square, bordered on two sides by chequers, encloses four guilloche squares, two with a duplex knot and two with multi-coloured chequers.

Illustration Fowler (1796-1818) appendix ii nos 10-11

SWALCLIFFE, Oxon
SP 3938   f 1926   Covered over in situ

Excavations over an area of 60 acres suggest that this is probably a scattered settlement with no defences. The swastika patterned border of a rectangular

pavement has been discovered
No published illustration   Reference VCH Oxfordshire I (1939) 308

TARRANT HINTON, Dorset
ST 9211

A Romano-British settlement above the village has produced large quantities
of tesserae and some simple mosaics.
a. f 1845
'A narrow passage, or corridor, was opened and followed to its termination,
where on each side was a doorway leading into two small apartments,
about five and a half or six feet square.' At least one of these rooms had
two concentric red rectangles with a red central stripe on a white ground.
*Illustration Shipp, W Dorsetshire 3 (1862) 28 ms in Dorset County Museum,
Dorchester*
b. Building I   f 1969   covered over in situ
A corridor has a central panel of chevron pattern in red on a white ground.
*Illustration Tanner, R M & Giles, A G Excavations at Barton Field,
Tarrant Hinton, Dorset (1971) pl IV*

TATWORTH (South Chard), Somerset
ST 3205   4th cent (?)   f 1965

A fragment of grey swastika pattern on a red ground.
No published illustration   Reference SDNQ XXVIII (1960-7) 279

THENFORD, Northants
SP 5241   4th cent (?)   f 1971

Remains of a villa and a tessellated pavement had been found in the last
century and excavations on the site have so far revealed a narrow room with a
mosaic divided by guilloche into three square panels. In the centre is a guilloche
bordered medallion framing a remarkably vivacious girl (?) with long hair,
bright eyes and parted lips, wearing either a cloak or a red cap with red
ribbons hanging over the hair and shoulders, and carrying a leafy twig; in each
spandrel is a crudely executed ivy leaf (?). This central square is flanked by
two panels, one of peltae pattern and the other of guilloche mat, a motif
which appears in a number of probable 4th century mosaics in Gloucestershire.
*Illustration in forthcoming publication   Reference VCH Northamptonshire I
(1902) 201*

THISTLETON DYER, Rutland
SK 9117   4th cent   Lost

A scattered settlement with a number of interesting buildings, but with no defences.

a. f 1960

In a winged corridor house with farm buildings, two rooms had mosaics in red, white and blue.

Reference JRS LI (1961) 175

b. f 1964

Three circular temples were found, one of which had a mosaic floor.

Reference JRS LV (1965) 207

THRUXTON, Hants
SU 2946   4th cent (?)   f 1823   In British Museum, London

When discovered this was a very fine mosaic with a central roundel, now lost, containing a muscular Bacchus holding a thyrsus and wine cup, and reclining on a puny leopard; vine leaves grow like trees on either side. A wide border is divided by guilloche into eight small panels, each containing the head of a little man wearing a Phrygian cap. In each spandrel is a female representation of one of the Seasons, with leaves and tendrils springing from her shoulders. Of the Latin inscriptions in panels on two sides of the mosaic, one was almost totally destroyed and the other, which may have been the artists' signatures, read 'Quintus Natalius Natallinus et Bodeni . . . '. The outer border has a frieze of swastikas and diamonds in simple outline.

Illustration Smith, D J (1969) pl 3.9

TIXOVER, Rutland
SK 9801   4th cent (?)

Several mosaics were found in a partially excavated villa.

a. f 1932

A grid of red squares on a white ground.

b. f 1932

Interlaced octagons, each with a central square, all executed in red on a white ground with an outer border of blue.

c. f 1959

Another grid of squares in red on a white ground may be the same as that found in 1932

Reference TLAHS XLVI (1970-1)

TOCKINGTON PARK, Glos
ST 6285   4th cent   exc 1887   Covered over in situ

Although a mosaic in this villa was first found in 1787 it was covered over again and forgotten until its rediscovery a hundred years later.
a. (Room II)
A small narrow room with a panel of involved swastika pattern.
Illustration TBGAS XII (1888) pl V fig 3
b. (Room III)
A guilloche bordered square encloses a stylised flower with four ivy leaf petals.
Illustrations TBGAS XII (1888) pl V figs 1-2
c. (Room IX)
A striking border of swastika pattern encloses a large saltire, the central medallion framing a flower with four ivy leaf petals, and the arms of the cross symmetrically decorated with swastika lozenges and pelta urns with convolutes.
Illustration TBGAS XII (1888) pl VI
d. (Room XII)
Basically an all-over pattern of interlaced guilloche squares and saltires fitted into a square, in the same manner as in the mosaic found at The Market in Gloucester. Central interlaced squares enclose a medallion holding a 'sunflower' with a duplex knot in the centre, while segmented squares in each corner frame, alternately, pelta urns with convolutes and lotus urns, the latter flanked by minute peltae. The four segmented saltires have rectangular panels of guilloche mat and ivy leaf scroll and the arms of the crosses are decorated with geometric devices, including ivy leaves, twists of guilloche and duplex knots.
Illustration TBGAS XII (1888) pl VII
e. (Corridor XXIII)
A long corridor of involved swastika pattern.
Illustration TBGAS XII (1888) pl VIII fig 2

TOTTERNHOE, Beds
SP 9920   4th cent   f 1954

A courtyard villa with several white tessellated floors, some bordered with grey, and a fragment of guilloche borders.
Illustration Matthews, C L Ancient Dunstable (Dunstable 1963) pl VIa

TWYFORD, Hants
SU 4824   f 1958

The bath suite of a courtyard villa was found in 1891 and re-excavations in

149

1958 revealed a fragment of mosaic showing borders of stepped triangles and chequers.
No published illustration Reference PSAL XIV (1891) 11

UFFINGTON see WOOLSTONE

VERULAMIUM see ST ALBANS

WADEFORD see COMBE ST NICHOLAS

WADFIELD (Sudeley Manor), Glos
SP 0226   4th cent (?)   f 1863   Roofed over on site

This attractive pavement was said to have been taken up and relaid in a greenhouse at Sudeley Castle, but is at present in a shed on the site. It has been restored and, despite recent neglect, is in surprisingly good condition. The mosaic is composed of a grid pattern with a central stylised flower framed by an unusual wreath of ivy leaves, similar to one in Room LXIV at Lydney, and with little urns and tendrils in the spandrels. Each rectangular panel holds a diamond with various arrangements of ivy leaves, lotus flowers and hearts, which also fill one of the corners, a stylised flower occupying the other.
Illustration Dent, E M Annals of Winchcombe & Sudeley (1877) 13

WALTON HEATH, Surrey
TQ 2353   2nd cent (?)   f 1856   Lost   plate 3A

A building, first found in 1772, had a number of red tessellated pavements and one mosaic with borders of swastikas and of an unusual lotus flower and ivy leaf scroll, the leaves being without stems and detached. A central square holds a guilloche bordered medallion framing an urn, decorated with a twist of guilloche, and with the most peculiar handles and a small foot. A square of guilloche mat occupies each corner of the mosaic and semi-circles on the sides hold segmented stylised flowers.
Illustration Drawing in the Haverfield Collection, Ashmolean Museum, Oxford   Reference Morgan (1886) 208

WANSTEAD PARK, Essex
TQ 4187   f 1715   Lost

A villa with 'A Roman pavement was discovered in Wanstead Park; that it was immediately destroyed by digging holes through it, for planting an avenue of trees . . . But, from the account I got from Mr Holt, the then surveyor of the works, I found that there was the figure of a man on horse-back plainly to be

seen in the centre, with several borders of wreathed work and ornaments, as are usually in these kinds of pavements.' If this was a lone figure it is more likely to have been Bacchus on a panther than a man on horseback.
Reference Arch I (1779) 73

WATER NEWTON see CHESTERTON

WELL, Yorks
SE 2681   2nd cent

Excavations on this small single corridor house, situated near a spring, have shown no trace of agricultural activities and it has been suggested that this may have been the house of a priest.
a. f 1859   In Well Church
   A corner of a mosaic with an outer border of white meander pattern.
   Illustration Gilyard-Beer (1951) pl IXa
b. f 1951
   A fragment of ivy leaf scroll from one of the rooms was found thrown into a bath
   Illustration Gilyard-Beer (1951) pl VIII

WELLOW, Somerset
ST 7258   Lost   Coloured drawings in Somerset County Museum, Taunton

A rich courtyard villa with a number of mosaic pavements, one of which was first found in 1685. Further excavations by various people went on for many years, resulting in numerous descriptions and illustrations which would appear to have been more colourful than accurate.
a. (Room A)   f 1685
   According to a reconstruction made from several sources, the VCH shows a complicated and asymmetric composition with interlaced guilloche squares framing a medallion supposed to have held figures; two peacocks flanking an urn are in one corner and two rectangular panels show lions (?) prancing amongst leafy tendrils. The rest of the ground is filled with panels of chequers, peltae, basket-work and so on. The two 'lions' are so similar to the two spotted dogs in pavement b. that one wonders whether they were included here in error. The second version is even more asymmetric and has one peacock in a triangle and a dog (?) under a spreading branch of a tree; whilst yet a third illustration is of part of the border only.
   Illustrations VCH Somerset I (1906) fig 71 & Vetusta Monumenta I (1747) pl 50 (alternative version)
b. (Room B)   f 1737

151

The swastika pattern dominates this mosaic, forming the border and, in guilloche, enclosing five small squares with duplex knots and geometric devices. Two long rectangular panels hold playful spotted dogs amongst leafy tendrils.

Illustrations VCH Somerset I (1906) fig 72 & Vetusta Monumenta I (1747) pl 51

c. (Room C)   f 1737

A narrow room or corridor mosaic is divided into five rectangles, the central panel having concentric octagons with uneven sides enclosing stylised flowers, flanked by peltae pattern and then by interlaced octagons.

Illustration Vetusta Monumenta I (1747) pl 52

d. (Room D)   f 1807

Another narrow room or corridor mosaic is divided into three panels. In the centre are interlaced circles enclosing small squares, flanked by panels of shaded bisected squares.

Illustration Drawing in Somerset County Museum, Taunton

e. (Corridor M)

Small chequers are bordered by large squares in two colours.

Illustration Plan in Somerset County Museum, Taunton

WEMBERHAM see YATTON

WEST DEAN, Hants
SU 2527   f 1741

Sporadic excavations took place over a period of one hundred years, revealing a large villa extending into Wiltshire. Unfortunately, only fragments of mosaic were found which, judging by coloured drawings, were probably of particularly high quality and of great interest.

a. f 1741   Lost

A square panel holds a roundel of shaded scale pattern with a small four-petalled white flower in the centre. It had plain red and white borders, apparently enclosing a rectangle, and one end of the room had uneven red and white stripes. The patterned part of the floor was taken up and exhibited to the public in public houses, being known as the 'Travelled Pavement'.

Illustrations JBAA Winchester Volume (1846) pl 8 figs 1-2

b. f 1845   Coloured drawing exhibited in Salisbury Museum

A number of border fragments with some interesting motifs.

i.   A frieze of peltae and a wreath of lutus flowers.

ii. Four rows of dog's tooth triangles.

iii. A partially opened fan.

iv. Two bands of lotus flower wreath.

v. A variation of the scroll of guilloche bordered circles, the circles, enclosing open fans, alternating with loops round peltae with spirals.

Illustration JBAA Winchester Volume (1846) pl 8

c. A square central panel with a two-handled urn in a guilloche medallion.

Reference JBAA Winchester Volume (1846) 239

d. A floor of chequer-board design.

Reference WAM XXII (1885) 243

WESTLAND (Yeovil), Somerset

ST 5415   4th cent   f 1927

A villa, or a group of villas, with a number of tessellated and simple geometric mosaic floors.

a. (Room 2)   In Wyndham Museum, Yeovil
   A fragment of guilloche with borders of stepped triangles.

b. (Room 4)
   A strip of swastika pattern in blue on white.
   Illustration Drawing in Wyndham Museum, Yeovil

c. (Room 6)
   A wide border of white swastika pattern enclosing small concentric squares with a border of triangles arranged so as to form a Maltese cross.
   Illustration PSANHS LXXIV (1928) pl C fig 1

d. (Room 10)   In Municipal Buildings, Yeovil
   A plain red grid on a black ground.
   Illustration PSANHS LXXIV (1928) pl C fig 2

e. (Room 23)
   Concentric squares arranged haphazardly on a white ground.
   Illustration Photograph in Wyndham Museum, Yeovil

WEST MARDEN (Watergates Hanger), Sussex

SU 7712   f 1895

A fragment of coarse red and white tesserae 'forming an elaborate pattern, a variety of the labyrinth or Greek fret.'

Reference SxAC XL (1896) 283

WEST MEON, Hants

SU 6324   f 1904

A small villa with several tessellated floors and two good mosaics.

a. (Room 3)
   A very fragmentary mosaic is divided by heavy guilloche braiding into a

153

square flanked by two rectangular panels. Interlaced guilloche squares have a lotus bud in each corner and one panel has a pattern of two-coloured triangles.
Illustration Arch J LXIV (1907) pl VII
b. (Room 4)
Concentric squares within a rectangle enclose concentric circles framing a duplex knot, all in red and white.
Illustration Arch J LXIV (1907) pl VI

WEST MERSEA, Essex
TM 0012

This appears to have been the site of a large villa, various tessellated and mosaic pavements having been found under the church and churchyard and in the garden of West Mersea Hall.
a. f 1730
Described by Cromwell Mortimer, and shown in Salmon's *History of Essex* (1739), as being rectangular, with a stylised flower in each corner, and with a central guilloche bordered rectangle containing two rows of three stylised flowers flanking a grid of diamonds.
Illustration VCH Essex III (1963) pl XXIIIb
b. f 1767
Judging from a contemporary drawing, this may have been a grid pattern mosaic, since the surviving fragment shows square and rectangular panels with stylised flowers and guilloche.
Illustration VCH Essex III (1963) pl XXIIIa
c. f 1956
A fragment has a large guilloche swastika in the corner, the arms framing panels, one of which contains a foliate scroll; in the centre two guilloche panels have an unusual border of duplex knots in diamonds. This is thought to be the same mosaic as the one found in 1730, but a reconstruction of the pattern based on the 1956 drawing and the following muddled description from Salmon's *History of Essex* seem to indicate a different pavement: 'The Doctor conjectures, that the whole pavement was of an oblong rectangular Form, extending twenty-one Foot and half from N. to S., and 18½ E - W having at each angle the blue and red wreaths interwoven; next to them, two of the square white spaces with the large rose in each on the N. and S. side, with an oblong white space between in the middle of each side. On E. and W. sides are the fretworks with ivy leaves repeated on each side the white space in the middle of each of these sides. Three of the lesser squares in a row on the W. side and 3 on the E. side. All intermediate spaces being filled with Lozenges and triangles.'

Illustration VCH Essex III (1963) pl XXII   Reference Salmon, N History of Essex (1739) 435

WEYMOUTH (Newberry Road), Dorset
SY 6778   f 1902   Fragments stored in Dorset County Museum, Dorchester

A fragment of mosaic belonging to a villa (?) overlooking the estuary of the River Wey, was found and brought to the Museum in Dorchester. It has borders of stepped triangles, guilloche and bright red and yellow and black and white chequers, unusually vivid in colour for a mosaic in Britain.
Illustration PDNHAS 85 (1963) fig 2
2. see also PRESTON

WHATLEY see NUNNEY

WHITTINGTON COURT, Glos
SP 0120   4th cent   f 1948

During the 4th century an older villa on this site was rebuilt and then enlarged; a number of coarse but interesting mosaic floors were laid and of these the patterns of five have survived.
a. (Room I)
   The mosaic floor in an apsed room has an awkward rectangular guilloche panel containing a five-sided guilloche bordered lozenge, with two small duplex knots and an arrangement of ivy leaves in two corners. Two borders have a foliate scroll and in the apex of the apse is a duplex knot flanked by two stemless ivy leaves surrounded by flowing lines.
   Illustrations TBGAS LXXI (1952) pls VII and VIII a & b
b. (Room III)
   A striking but simple pattern executed in coarse tesserae has large concentric circles containing two plain interlaced squares with intersecting lines forming a 'union jack'. Panels on two sides have a grid framing smaller squares.
   Illustration TBGAS LXXI (1952) pl I
c. (Room V)
   A guilloche bordered square contains a large saltire, the arms formed of perspective boxes framing small stemless ivy leaves, and the central medallion holding a duplex knot.
   Illustration TBGAS LXXI (1952) pl II
d. (Room X)
   Most of the floor of this, the largest room in the villa, had been destroyed, but enough remained to show that there had been panels of Greek key pattern and one of chequers round a guilloche bordered centre.

Illustration TBGAS LXXI (1952) pl VIb and fig 2 (plan)

e. (Corridor II)

An attractive and ambitious mosaic divided into three parts with, in the centre, a guilloche roundel framing a duplex knot, flanked by chequers; on one side of this is an all-over peltae pattern and on the other side perspective box pattern framing a square with a duplex knot.

Illustrations TBGAS LXXI (1952) pls III, IV and p 13

WHITTLEBURY (The Gullet), Northants

SP 7344   f 1850

Partial excavations of this villa were sparsely recorded and the mosaic with a female bust, said to have been taken to Windsor Castle, cannot be traced.

a. plate 14A

A coarsely executed square panel in the middle of the floor shows the bust of a winged female, wearing a wreath and probably holding a spray of leaves, which may represent the goddess Victoria.

Illustration JBAA VII (1852) pl XI

b. A mosaic panel in the porch appears to have had a pattern of red crosses with borders of guilloche and fret or chequers in red and grey.

References JBAA VII (1852) 107 & VCH Northamptonshire I (1902) 199

c. A grid of squares outlined in red with a square of white at each intersection.

Reference JBAA VI (1851) 73

WHITTON (Ipswich), Suffolk

TM 1446   2nd cent   f 1854   In Ipswich Museum

a. A small central square, contents destroyed, has seven narrow borders, some being of unusual design and including diamonds, triangles with curved sides, parallelograms bisected to form two-coloured triangles and ovals which are similar to the border of one panel at Gayton Thorpe in Norfolk.

Illustration PSIA XXI (1931-3) 246

b. Interlaced octagons enclosing a small square, all in white on a red ground.

Illustration PSIA XXI (1931-3) 247

WIDFORD (St Oswald's Church), Oxon

SP 2712   f 1904   Fragment on view in situ

During the restoration of the church, fragments of a mosaic pavement were found under the floor of the chancel. Interlaced octagons each contain four lozenges, with a red centre, round a central hollow box, all in black on white.

Illustration Ant J XLVII (1967) pl XXa

WIGGINTON, Oxon
SP 3933   4th cent   f 1824

Part of a large house with a number of mosaic and tessellated floors was
found in 1824 and re-excavated in 1965. Some pieces of mosaic of geometric
pattern were found in the hypocaust of Room 4 and in Room 16.

a. (Room 1)
   An outer border of swastikas enclosing panels of guilloche, and on at least
   one side a scroll of guilloche bordered circles, frame a very fragmentary
   pattern, possibly composed of all-over interlaced guilloche squares and
   segmented saltires. At least one pair of segmented interlaced guilloche
   squares in the corner holds a fluted urn, and one oblong panel formed by
   a segmented saltire frames a lotus wreath.
   No published illustration   Reference JRS LVI (1966) 208

b. (Room 3)
   A fragmentary border of guilloche and squares.
   No published illustration

c. (Room 7)
   Of a large square mosaic only fragments of the borders survive, showing
   swastikas enclosing panels of peltae, diamonds and squares.
   No published illustration

d. (Room 14)   f 1824   Covered over in situ
   A three-sided apse with borders of guilloche and of swastikas holding
   panels of guilloche, frames a small panel with an unusual urn, from the
   base of which flows an ivy leaf tendril scroll.
   Illustration Beesley (1848) pl XI

WINCHCOMBE see WADFIELD

WINCHESTER *(Venta Belgarum)*, Hants
SU 4829

A cantonal capital with fortifications enclosing an area of 138 acres, which
may have been divided by a grid of streets into 40 *insulae*, but it is possible
that the west end of the town was never fully developed.

1. Dome Alley   f 1880   Fragment in porch of the Deanery, Winchester
A small but good fragment of a mosaic found in the Canon's garden, shows a
corner with guilloche and ivy leaves and one attractive border of ivy leaf
scroll.
Reference JBAA XXXVI (1880) 444

2. Little Minster Street   f 1878   In Winchester City Museum   plate 9B
This pavement was said to have been 'a large and elaborate mosaic which had
for its general subject a pattern of interlacing squares with heads and figures

157

like Bramdean.' From the fragment preserved in the museum, one can see that this was probably an all-over pattern of saltires and interlaced guilloche squares, the latter segmented along the sides of the mosaic, and one framing a lively dolphin. The only surviving saltire has a star in a central square and the arms of the cross are decorated with lotus flowers, a dolphin and geometric devices. Remains of a whole medallion in interlaced guilloche squares may well have held a bust.

Reference VCH Hampshire I (1900) 288

3. Middle Brook Street   f 1953   Stored in Winchester City Museum

A fragment of a corridor with panels of swastikas and concentric squares.

Illustration PPHFC XVIII (1954) pl II

4. St Georges Street   circa AD 200   f 1954   Fragments in Winchester City Museum

A badly damaged but attractive pavement has a large guilloche bordered saltire, the central medallion destroyed. One arm of the cross is decorated with a well-proportioned fluted urn and another has a little bowl with an arrangement of ivy leaves. Two (?) semi-circles frame cornucopiae, one corner has a small urn and another a six-petalled flower bud or a half open fan.

Illustration JRS XLIX (1959) pl XVI

WINGHAM, Kent
TR 2457   f 1881

Mosaics from the bath house of a villa, found in 1881, were re-excavated in 1965 and found to be in fairly good condition.

a. (Room 1)

A plunge bath with the walls tessellated in white and grey.

b. (Room 2)

A simple all-over pattern of dark hourglass triangles arranged so as to form large and small white squares.

c. (Room 3)

An all-over pattern of swastikas enclosing small squares.

Illustration Arch Cant XIV (1882) 136

WINTERTON, Lincs
SE 9318

A series of mosaic pavements were found in the 18th century and engraved by William Fowler. Re-excavations, starting in 1958, showed the mosaics to have been much damaged, but it was nevertheless possible to photograph and draw the remains in situ. The earlier illustrations are thus shown to have been accurate for the general design and themes, but for the details it is well worth consulting David Neal's version and then comparing it with Fowler's, the

15A
(*right*) Nunney,
Somerset. Bust
with mural crown
and cornucopia.
(From a coloured
drawing in
Somerset County
Museum, Taunton)

15B
(*left*) Great
Witcombe,
Gloucestershire
(Room 6). Marine
scatter. (From a
coloured drawing
in the Society of
Antiquaries of
London)

16A
(*left*) Stonesfield,
Oxfordshire
(Room A). Saltire.
(From a coloured
drawing in the
Society of
Antiquaries of
London)

16B
(*right*) Wynford
Eagle, Dorset.
Geometric with
dolphins.
(Photograph in
Dorset County
Museum,
Dorchester)

latter's easily accessible in *The Roman Villa in Britain* edited by A L F Rivet.
a. f circa 1747

A rectangular pavement, bordered by alternate lozenges and chequers, has two panels of white meander with guilloche filling each loop, flanking a large circle. A central octagon encloses a crudely drawn figure of Orpheus, each of eight radiating panels holds a toy-like animal, and a two-handled urn occupies each outer corner.

Illustrations Smith, D J (1969) pl 3.17 & photograph of David Neal's drawing in Dept of the Environment

b. f circa 1747   Lost

A fragment with chequered borders has two panels, one enclosing a lozenge bordered medallion and the other a hunted stag.

Illustration Smith, D J (1969) pl 3.17

c. f circa 1747   Reconstructed fragment in Civic Centre, Scunthorpe

A long narrow pavement has two large panels of shaded interlaced circles and two small panels of scale pattern flanking a square containing a circle. Within this, two interlaced squares frame a medallion with a female, probably Ceres, carrying a sheaf of corn (?).

Illustration Smith, D J (1969) pl 3.17

d. f circa 1747   Lost

A fragment of perspective box pattern decorated with flowers was drawn by Fowler and included with the Winterton illustrations, but it is now thought to be a piece of the Roxby mosaic.

Illustration Smith, D J (1969) pl 3.17

e. f 1797   Restored fragment in Scunthorpe Museum

In a central guilloche bordered circle, between two panels of guilloche mat, is the crudely drawn bust of Abundantia holding a cornucopia filled with fruit. In the four spandrels are curiously shaped peltae.

Illustration Smith, D J (1969) 3.18

f. f 1958   2nd cent (?)

Small fragments found on the site have been reconstructed in a drawing to show perspective boxes with plain sides shaded to give a three-dimensional impression, a treatment which is unique in Britain.

Illustration Photograph of a drawing by David Neal in Dept of the Environment

g. f 1964   2nd cent (?)

A fragment of a somewhat clumsy foliate scroll.

Illustration Photograph of a drawing by David Neal in Dept of the Environment

h. f 1958   2nd cent (?)

A fragment of Greek key swastikas and rectangles (?)

Illustration Photograph of a drawing by David Neal in Dept of the Environment

WITHINGTON, Glos
SP 0314   4th cent (?)   f 1811

A villa with a number of simple mosaic pavements, and one of some sophistication, all drawn by Samuel Lysons.

a. A narrow rectangle of interlaced octagons enclosing quatrefoils and chequers.
Illustration Lysons II (1817) pl XIX fig A

b. A small square of chequers.
Illustration Lysons II (1817) pl XIX fig B

c. A rectangle is divided into three panels; in the centre a border of guilloche framing a small rectangle of interlaced circles is flanked by squares of perspective box pattern.
Illustration Lysons II (1817) pl XIX fig C

d. Fragments in Bristol City Museum and in British Museum, London
A long rectangular room has a mosaic divided by guilloche into five panels A large circle within a square has a central medallion framing Orpheus playing to a fox (?) on his lyre. Bounding round the circle are various beasts, interspersed with curious little trees with lotus flowers instead of leaves. On two sides are narrow panels, one with two (?) peacocks flanking an urn and the other with six naturalistic birds on either side of an object resembling a floral wheel. The next two panels are irregular rectangles, probably inserted at a later date by a different mosaicist. The first holds Neptune, two dolphins sprouting from his beard, and sea-beasts, dolphins, flowers and trees crammed in around him. The next panel shows only the hind legs of a beast being followed by the forelegs of a horse, interpreted by Samuel Lysons as a lion hunt. The fourth panel has a dolphin and a sea-beast (?), and the fifth a narrow strip of peltae pattern.
Illustrations Smith, D J (1969) pl 3.11 & Lysons II (1817) pl XIX fig D

e. A long room or corridor has an all-over pattern of swastikas enclosing bisected squares and, in the centre (?) where there is an apse, this pattern is interrupted by a square of guilloche mat leading to a square of pelta-duplex-swastikas and another guilloche mat.
Illustration Lysons II (1817) pl XIX fig E

f. A square of interlaced circles.
Illustration Lysons II (1817) pl XIX fig F

g. A long corridor with a narrow strip of swastikas in two colours.
Illustration Lysons II (1817) pl XIX fig G

h. Another corridor with plain squares composed of chequers, and rectangles holding concentric lozenges.
Illustration Lysons II (1817) pl XXI 2

WOODCHESTER, Glos
SO 8303   4th cent   Covered over in situ

A large and very sophisticated mosaic from a palatial villa was first found below the churchyard as early as 1695. The large mosaic was uncovered and drawn in 1722 by R. Bradley, and later by Samuel Lysons, who also excavated and drew a number of other pavements on this site in the late 18th century. A description of the mosaics may be found in *The Roman Villa at Woodchester* (1951) by M D Mann.

a. (Room 1)   f circa 1695   Covered over in situ, but periodically opened to view   Small fragment in British Museum, London
A large and richly decorated mosaic with a great number and variety of patterns packed into a cohesive and symmetric all-over design. It is too complicated to attempt a full description, but, basically, a large swastika bordered square holds another square, within which lie concentric circles, and finally an octagon. Bradley suggested that within this again were fishes swimming round a central medallion containing a 'starlike object'. Orpheus and a fox (?) break into the next frieze of birds of all sizes, which is separated from a circle of prowling beasts by guilloche and a wreath of leaves; outside these comes a heavy acanthus leaf scroll springing from a mask of Neptune. In each spandrel was the base of a pillar flanked by reclining water nymphs, each with a water urn, similar to the nymphs at Brantingham in Yorkshire. The wide border between the two squares is divided into symmetrically arranged geometric patterns, including perspective boxes, lozenge swastikas, medallions framing urns or stylised flowers, and squares of all-over swastika pattern.
Illustrations Smith, D J (1969) pl 3.13 & Lysons (1797) pl X

b. (Corridor 2)
i. A very long corridor is divided by guilloche into twenty-eight panels containing a variety of geometric designs, including swastika patterns and squares, guilloche mats, pelta-duplex-swastikas and perspective boxes.
Illustration Lysons (1797) pl XI
ii. Many fragments of mosaic were found lying in another length of this corridor, including a small piece of a guilloche bordered panel framing a naked man with a cloak or animal skin, and the head of a woman wearing her hair in a top knot, both with a nimbus.
Illustration Lysons (1797) pl XVI fig 2

c. (Room 3)
A large rectangle of guilloche mat bordered by bands of red.
Illustration Lysons (1797) pl XIII

d. (Room 5)
An effective band of swastikas in black on white with a border of red

163

tesserae.
Illustration Lysons (1797) pl XIIa

:. (Room 6)
A rectangular pavement with two guilloche bordered squares filled with swastika pattern enclosing small concentric squares.
Illustration Lysons (1797) pl XIV

f. (Room 8)
Alternate panels of guilloche mat and an unusual small labyrinth pattern.
Illustration Lysons (1797) pl XIIb

g. (Room 10)
A square with five guilloche bordered octagons is very fragmentary; in the only undamaged panel, two small naked boys, draped with scarves, hold aloft a basket of fruit and beneath them is the inscription *'Bonum Eventum'* ('Happiness to you'). Two panels hold dancing figures, probably Satyrs and Maenads, and in the fourth is part of another inscription *'Bene C[olite]'* ('Enjoy yourselves'). On one side is a scroll of flower buds springing from a central urn, and the whole is bordered by swastika pattern. This pavement has much in common with one of the mosaics found at Pitney in Somerset.
Illustrations Smith, D J (1969) pl 3.14 & Lysons (1797) pl XIX

h. (Room 12)
Fragments show a large circle, contents destroyed, in a square with the spandrels holding ivy or smilax leaves and tightly curled tendrils. A panel holds the heavy acanthus leaf scroll which is also found in the Orpheus pavement.
Illustrations Lysons (1797) pls XV and XVI fig 3

i. (Room 13)
A central square of interlaced circles is bordered by striking bands of red and white.
Illustration Lysons (1797) pl XVI fig 1

j. (Room 15)
A square of swastika pattern, enclosing panels of duplex knots, is flanked by two narrow panels with a line of triangles bordered by 'Z' pattern and wave crests.
Illustration Lysons (1797) pl XVII

k. (Room 18)
A border of swastika pattern encloses two guilloche bordered squares, one with an urn framed by pelta-duplex-swastikas, and the other with s small guilloche mat set in perspective boxes.
Illustration Lysons (1797) pl XVIII

l. (Room 19)
A very small room with an all-over pattern of chequers.

Illustration Lysons (1797) pl XXII fig 1

WOOLSTONE (Uffington), Berks
SU 2987

A building with a long corridor and two mosaic floors, one of key pattern, was first found in 1884. Re-excavation in 1955 revealed another tessellated corridor and a geometric mosaic.

a. f 1884

An attractive design of variously shaped panels frames stylised flowers, lotus wreath, foliate scroll and an arrangement of heart motifs. The general effect is reminiscent of a mosaic in Ashcroft Road, Cirencester.
Illustration Berks AJ 43 (1939) pl I

b. f 1955

A wide border of simple tendril scroll runs round a square, contents destroyed, with borders of stepped triangles and semi-circles.
Illustration Berks AJ 57 (1959) opp 84

WORPLESDON (Broadstreet Green), Surrey
SU 9651   f 1829

A passage running the length of a building had on one edge a border of very small tesserae, arranged in an uneven double wavy ribbon pattern in red and black. A report that it was relaid at Clandon Park appears to be incorrect.
Illustration Arch XXIII (1831) 398 and 400

WROXETER *(Viroconium Cornoviorum)*, Salop
SJ 5608

A *civitas* capital of some 180 acres was built on a site which had been chosen for strategic reasons as a military post. The modern village of Wroxeter, lying at the extreme southern end of *Viroconium,* occupies only a fraction of this area. Excavations have taken place sporadically since 1701, and the few mosaics found so far are of geometric design. One of the public baths was said to have had a cream-coloured tessellated floor and a guilloche patterned mosaic on the wall.

1. f 1706

A square mosaic with a clumsy stylised flower.
Illustration VCH Shropshire I (1908) fig 16

2. f 1734

A rectangular pavement has an apse entirely filled by a large shaded pelta, while the main part of the floor appears to have large shaded semi-circles round the sides and nothing in the middle.

Illustration Duke, T F ms p.34 in Soc of Ant of London
3. f 1827 Lost
A drawing by T F Duke shows a rectangle with a large eight-pointed star enclosing a strange stylised flower within a central medallion, and four semi-circles each framing half a 'union jack'. Two panels have a scroll, unique in Britain, although it appears in frescoes in the Mediterranean area. The number of unusual features in this mosaic leads to speculation as to the accuracy of the drawing, and the existence of another illustration in the Shrewsbury museum does nothing to make Duke's version more convincing. The Shrewsbury drawing, which seems the more genuine of the two, could certainly be of yet another mosaic, but it is sufficiently similar to make this unlikely. The mosaic, which is fragmentary, shows interlaced guilloche squares enclosing a sixteen-petalled flower, a quarter-circle with a segmented stylised flower, and a scroll of guilloche bordered circles framing a small red medallion and a red and white quartered circle. The mosaic may have been composed of four pairs of interlaced guilloche squares with a central octagon enclosing a medallion.
Illustrations Arch J LIV (1897) pl II & Drawing in Rowley's House Museum Shrewsbury
4. f 1827 Fragment in Rowley's House Museum, Shrewsbury
A fragment, which may have come from Wroxeter, although there is no proof of this, appears to show a square enclosing a large circle within which are over-lapping medallions, one with a rainbow-shaded border and a red and black quartered centre, and the other probably bordered with guilloche. The design may well have been similar to that of the mosaic at Holcombe in Devon. The one surviving spandrel has a pelta urn with convolutes, and there is an adjacent panel with a duplex knot and a border of wave crests.
No published illustration
5. (Insula 5) f 1859 Fragment in Rowley's House Museum, Shrewsbury
A corridor in a public building was excavated and drawn in 1859, but when re-excavated in 1937 only a small fragment was found to have survived. The mosaic had a series of twenty-six panels, all filled with simple geometric patterns, such as chequers, triangles and 'L' shapes with borders of meander, Greek key and guilloche.
Illustrations Arch J LIV (1897) pl III & Arch LXXXVIII (1938) pl LXVc

WYNFORD EAGLE, Dorset
SY 5795 4th cent (?) f circa 1856 Covered over in situ plate 16B

A mosaic pavement, some sixty feet long, was found in the orchard of Wynford House. As far as can be seen from the area re-excavated in 1935, it is divided by guilloche into octagons containing medallions, with contents destroyed, and corner panels each framing a lively dolphin with a curly tail. A long narrow border panel on one side of the mosaic has an unusual arrangement of

leaves in staggered pairs on both sides of a central band.
Illustration Photograph in Dorset County Museum, Dorchester   Reference RCHM Dorset I (1952) 269

YARCHESTER (Much Wenlock), Salop
SJ 6000   4th cent (?)   f 1957   Covered over in situ

Very limited excavations of a corridor villa revealed a row of rooms with a large apse and a mosaic pavement. The main part of the floor, which was badly damaged, has a broad border of guilloche mat enclosing four pairs of interlaced guilloche squares, possibly similar to the design of a mosaic found in The Avenue (The Leauses), Cirencester. One surviving central medallion has an unusual border of Greek key pattern and one outer corner has a single ivy leaf with tendrils, both these features being very similar to those in a mosaic at Bratton Seymour in Somerset. A panel of diamonds leads to the curved apse, which has a square with a border of four large swastikas enclosing four panels of guilloche. The large central guilloche bordered medallion frames an eight-petalled 'sunflower', the design being very similar to those of the 4th century mosaics found in Insula XXVII.3 at Verulamium and in a room in the bath suite at Lufton in Somerset, although the latter has some subtle variations.
Illustrations Shropshire Magazine September 1957 23 and photographs in Rowley's House Museum, Shrewsbury

YATTON (Wemberham), Somerset
ST 4065   f 1884

A villa found here lies on low, marshy ground traversed by the present course of the River Yeo. A number of rooms had mosaic and tessellated floors with patterns which included borders of swastikas and scrolls.
a. (Room A)
   A central roundel frames a large foliate cross with lotus buds on stalks between the arms; the square of 'Z' pattern holding this medallion is interlaced with a square of chequers and is, in its turn, framed by a circle of 'Z' pattern within another square; in the spandrels are large lotus buds with tendrils. This outer square lies within a large circle which touches the outer edge of the mosaic, and the semi-circular panels, formed thereby, hold attractive lotus bud and acanthus leaf sprays. Each of the outer spandrels has a stylised flower flanked by truncated cornucopiae.
   Illustration VCH Somerset I (1906) fig 67
b. (Room B)
   A small fragment probably shows one arm of a guilloche saltire, decorated with a duplex knot. The only surviving quarter-circle has a heart and there are indications that the semi-circles held sprays of leaves.
   Illustration PSANHS XXXI (1886) 70

167

YEOVIL see WESTLAND

YORK *(Eburacum)*, Yorks
SE 6052

A military fortress and a *colonia* grew up side by side, the latter probably covering about 100 acres. Houses were also built along the approach road outside the town.

1. Cherry Hill   f circa 1850   Lost

A drawing, the original of which is now lost, shows a fragment with an eight-pointed star, a lotus flower and a smilax leaf within a plaited border. On one side a panel of peltae pattern has an inset with an arrangement of lotus flowers and convoluted ivy leaves.

Illustration RCHM York I (1962) pl 23b

2. Micklegate Bar   f 1814   Lost   plate 5

A fascinating, if not particularly attractive mosaic is quite unique in Britain. Five octagons in a setting of variously decorated perspective boxes contain joints of venison with sprays of leaves or herbs, and in the centre there are two deer. The figured area of the pavement is surrounded by a broad border of the unusual swastika pattern, which is also found at Aldborough, and a narrower outer border with squares and little twists of guilloche.

Illustration RCHM York I (1962) pl 23

3. Toft Green

a. f 1840   In Yorkshire Museum, York
   A fragment showing a lively sea-cow.
   Illustration RCHM York I (1962) pl 22

b. (Room 2)   f 1853   In Yorkshire Museum, York
   The arms of four large guilloche swastikas enclose busts of the Seasons; Spring with a bird on her shoulder, Summer with a harvest rake, Autumn with a bunch of grapes and Winter with a leafless twig. In the central fragmentary square, the snakes on the head of Medusa are just recognisable.
   Illustration RCHM York I (1962) pl 24

c. (Room 3)   f 1853   Fragment in Yorkshire Museum, York
   A fragment of grid pattern.
   Illustration RCHM York I (1962) pl 22

d. (Room 4)   f 1853   One medallion in Yorkshire Museum, York
   A grid of five guilloche bordered medallions with roughly drawn stylised flowers, each circle being framed by eight narrow geometric panels. A more sophisticated version of this method of forming a frame can be found in a mosaic at Grately in Hampshire.
   Illustration RCHM York I (1962) pl 23a

GLOSSARY

ABRAXAS/ABRASAX   A Gnostic power, usually represented with the head of a fowl, the arms and bust of a man and the body terminating in the tail of a serpent.

ABUNDANTIA (Roman)   Personification of prosperity and good fortune. In artistic representations, holds a cornucopia.

ACANTHUS   *Acanthacaea montanus*. Genus of prickly plants found in southern Europe and Asia Minor. Conventional representation of leaf first used in art by the Greeks.

ACTAEON (Greek)   A famous huntsman and Greek hero. He surprised Artemis bathing naked and as a punishment was transformed into a stag and devoured by his own hounds.

AENEAS   Trojan Hero in Virgil's *Aeneid* and legendary ancestor of the Romans. Fought at Troy and when it fell in flames, escaped with his old father and his son Ascanius. With the surviving Trojans he eventually sailed with the fleet for Italy, but had many adventures on the way. A storm drove his ship ashore near Carthage, where Dido fell passionately in love with him, a love which he appears to have reciprocated, but on the orders of Jupiter he sailed away forever. Dido then committed suicide.

AMBROSIA   A Maenad attacked by Lycurgus.

AMPHORA   A two-handled vessel for holding wine, oil etc.

171

ANDROMEDA (Greek)

Andromeda was chained to a rock as a sacrifice to a hideous sea-beast. Perseus found her, killed the monster and married her.

ANTAEUS (Greek)

Son of Neptune and Terra. A champion wrestler, he derived renewed strength from his mother, Earth, every time he was thrown to the ground. Finally met his match when Hercules held him in the air and crushed him to death.

APHRODITE

See Venus.

APOLLO (Greek & Roman)

God of the sun, music and poetry. In art a beautiful youth, usually naked save for a cloak, and carrying bow and arrows or a lyre. He was challenged by Marsyas to a musical contest, which he won, and in punishment for his temerity, Marsyas was skinned alive.

APSE

A semi-circular or polygonal recess in a building.

ARES

See Mars.

ARTEMIS (Greek)

Diana (Roman). Goddess of hunting and of the moon. As the former is shown wearing a short tunic and sandals, carrying a bow and arrows and accompanied by a hound; as the latter is dressed in a long robe, her head surmounted by a crescent moon.

ATHENE

See Minerva.

AWNING PATTERN

BACCHAE & BACCHANTES

See Maenads.

BACCHUS (Roman)

Dionysus (Greek). God of wine. Son of Zeus and Semele. Associated with all ecstatic states, particularly that induced by wine. Maenads and

Satyrs were his followers. In art usually appears as a young man crowned with leaves and holding a drinking cup, naked apart from a panther skin, and often reclining on a panther or a tiger.

BEAD AND REEL

BELLEROPHON (Greek)

Tamed Pegasus, the winged horse, with a golden bridle. Rejected the advances of the Queen of Argos, who then falsely accused him and sent him to the King of Lycia with a sealed message asking for his own death. The King despatched him to kill the monster, Chimaera, which he achieved riding on Pegasus, and as a reward was finally given the King's daughter in marriage.

BONUS EVENTUS (Roman)

Male counterpart of Fortuna, being the god responsible for success in all enterprises.

BRICK PATTERN

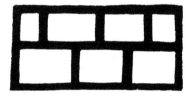

CADMUS (Greek)

A Greek hero who fetched water from a spring sacred to the god of War, slew the attendant serpent or dragon, and from its teeth, which he scattered on the ground, sprang the men of Thebes.

CADUCEUS

The winged, serpent-entwined staff of Mercury.

173

CANTHARUS — An urn or wine mixing bowl with two handles. See urn.

CASTELLATED PATTERN

CELLA — The inner room or shrine of a temple.

CENTAUR — A creature with the body and legs of a horse and the torso of a man.

CENTAUR, SEA — A centaur with the body of a man, the front legs of a horse and the tail of a fish.

CERES (Roman) — Demeter (Greek). Mother of the earth and goddess of agriculture. In art often seen carrying ears of corn or a basket of fruit. Taught agriculture to Triptolemus and gave him the tools.

CHAIN PATTERN

CHEQUERS (CHESSBOARD)

CHEVRON PATTERN

CHIMAERA — A monster in Greek mythology. Has the head of a lion, the tail of a serpent and a goat's head growing out of its back. See also Bellerophon.

CHI-RHO

Monogram of the first two letters of Christ's name in Greek, XPIC TOC, from which was derived the Christian cross.

CIRCLES, INTERLACED

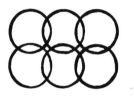

CIRCUS

A long, narrow race course, divided by a low wall or *spina*, at each end of which was a column to mark the turning point for the chariots in the race.

CIVITAS CAPITAL

The chief town of a tribal area or community and the seat of its administration, built according to a plan with a grid of streets, civic buildings, baths, temples and amphitheatres. The tribal name is usually added to that of the town.

COLONIA

A chartered settlement of Roman citizens; in Britain mainly retired legionaries who received a grant of land instead of money on leaving the army.

CONCH SHELL

A spiral marine shell used as a trumpet. Attribute of the Wind gods.

175

CONVOLUTE   Coil or spiral.

CORNUCOPIA   The horn of plenty, symbol of peace and abundance.

CROSS, MALTESE   A name wrongly applied to the cross *patée*.

CUPID (Roman)   Eros (Greek). God of love and son of Venus. A beautiful boy, often shown naked and with wings.

CUSHION-SHAPE

CYPARISSUS (Greek)   A youth, beloved of Apollo, accidentally killed a much loved stag. His distress was so great that Apollo transformed him into a Cypress tree.

DEMETER   See Ceres.

DENTIL BORDER

DIAMOND PATTERN

DIANA   See Artemis.

DIDO   Queen of Carthage. Committed suicide when deserted by her lover Aeneas. See also Aeneas.

DIONYSUS   See Bacchus.

DUPLEX KNOT   Compounded of two. Also known as Solomon's knot, guilloche knot, endless knot, single knot and lover's knot.

DUPLEX KNOT WITH PELTAE

177

EMBLEMA (TA)   A panel of mosaic executed in very small tesserae.

EROS   See Cupid.

EUROPA (Greek)   When Europa was picking flowers on the sea-shore, Zeus, who desired her, appeared in the form of a beautiful white bull. She caressed him, offered him flowers and then, seated on his back, was carried off across the sea to Crete.

FAN, CIRCULAR   Also known as an umbrella.

FAUN   See Satyr.

FLORA (Roman)   Goddess of flowers.

FLOWERS, STYLISED   These take many forms, from a simple four-petalled flower to one with petals formed of four lotus buds and four ivy leaves.

FOLIATE SPRAY

178

FORTUNA (Roman)

Tyche (Greek). The goddess of good fortune and female counterpart of Bonus Eventus. Worshipped under numerous titles as the protectress of cities and individual enterprises.

FRET

Straight lines joined at right angles. A word used to describe meander or swastika patterns.

GANYMEDE (Greek)

A Trojan prince, seized by Zeus in the guise of an eagle and carried to Olympus to be cup-bearer to the gods.

GLADIATORS

Professional combatants who fought to the death for public entertainment. The *Retiarius,* wearing armbands and an armoured plate on his left shoulder and equipped only with a net and a trident, with which he attempted to entangle and kill the *Secutor,* who was heavily armed.

GNOSTICISM

An obscure mystic philosophy compounded of Hebrew, Greek and Christian concepts, particularly popular in Egypt.

GREEK KEY PATTERN

GRID PATTERN

GRID OF SQUARES

GRIFFIN/GRYPHON   A fabulous creature with the head and wings of a bird and the body and legs of a lion.

GUILLOCHE   Ornamental bordering used in mosaics, composed of two or more twisted strands. Numerous strands form a GUILLOCHE MAT.

HELICON, MOUNT   Reputed home of the nine Greek Muses.

HELLENISM   Greek civilisation or culture.

HERA (Greek)   Juno (Roman). Wife of Zeus. Goddess of women. Often shown as a mature and majestic woman wearing a diadem and holding a sceptre and a pomegranate.

HERCULES (Roman)   Heracles (Greek). A hero personifying great physical strength, which enabled him to perform twelve superhuman labours. Is often represented nude, save for a lion's skin, and carrying a club.

HERMES   See Mercury.

HYPOCAUST   A room heating system in which a fire was kept burning in a furnace, usually built against an outer wall, the heat being circulated along channels running between pillars carrying the floor, drawn up chimney flues embedded in the walls and dispersed at roof level.

INSULA
In a town, the name given to the plots of ground delimited by the streets. In references the number of the *insula* (island) is given first, followed by the house and finally the room number.

IN SITU
In its original position. On the site.

JUNO
See Hera.

JUPITER or JOVE
(Roman)
Zeus (Greek). The supreme god to the Romans, as Zeus was to the Greeks. Worshipped in many forms, such as Jupiter Tonans, god of Storms and Thunder. As Zeus, in Greek mythology, he appeared to the mortals Semele, as lightning, Ganymede, as an eagle, and to Europa, as a white bull. In art is usually shown with thick curly hair and a beard. Represents Thursday, *dies Jovis.*

LABYRINTH PATTERN
A maze. A system of intricate winding paths or passages. The Cretan labyrinth was built by the Greek artificer, Daedalus, to imprison the Minotaur.

LOTUS FLOWER
Nymphaea Lotus (L). An Egyptian water lily, much used in stylised form for decoration in Greek and Roman art. Symbol of life and resurrection.

LOTUS WREATH or
SCROLL

LOZENGES — Eight lozenges form a star.

LUNA/DIANA (Roman) — Selene/Artemis (Greek). Goddess of the moon. Represents Monday, *dies lunae.*

LYCURGUS (Greek) — King of Thrace, who abolished the worship of Bacchus. In revenge he was driven mad by the god and in this condition mistook the Maenad, Ambrosia, for a vine and killed her with an axe.

MAENADS (Greek) — Female followers of Dionysus/Bacchus. Ran and danced in a frenzy carrying serpents, thyrsi or cymbals. Also known as Bacchae and Bacchantes.

MARS (Roman) — Ares (Greek). God of War. Wears armour and a helmet and carries a spear. Represents Tuesday, *dies Martis.*

MARSYAS (Greek) — A Phrygian Satyr. Picked up Athene's pipes and challenged Apollo to a musical contest. When he lost, he was flayed alive.

MEANDER PATTERN

MEDUSA (Greek) — One of the three Gorgons, such horrible monsters that to see them was to be turned to stone. Her head was cut off by Perseus and

182

given to Athene to put on her shield.

MERCURY (Roman)	Hermes (Greek). The Roman god of commerce, herald and messenger of the gods. Wears winged boots, hat and cloak and carries a caduceus and a purse. Represents Wednesday, *dies Mercurii*.
MINERVA (Roman)	Athene (Greek). Goddess of wisdom and of the arts and protectress of the state, in which role she is usually represented wearing armour, the head of Medusa on her breastplate or shield.
MINOTAUR	A monster having a human body and the head of a bull, was confined in the centre of the Cretan labyrinth where he devoured youths and maidens. Eventually killed by Theseus.
MUNICIPIUM	A chartered town, ranking below a *colonia* and above a *civitas* capital, the inhabitants of which had Roman citizenship but were governed by their own magistrates and laws.
MURAL CROWN	Usually a circlet of gold adorned with a series of turrets.

NEPTUNE (Roman)	Poseidon (Greek). God of the sea, his symbol a trident. Is often represented with a large beard and accompanied by fishes, dolphins and seaweed and with lobster claws growing from his head.
NEREIDS	Beautiful sea nymphs
NIKE (Greek	See Victoria

183

OCTAGONS,
INTERLACED

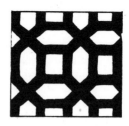

OLYMPUS, MOUNT	Home of the gods.
OPUS SIGNINUM	A floor of cement reinforced with pebbles or pieces of stone.
ORPHEUS	Legendary poet of the Greeks, personifying the power of music. Playing on his golden lyre, he charmed the wild beasts. Killed by the Maenads, his head and lyre were thrown into the river. It floated away to the sea crying out the name of his dead wife, the lovely nymph Eurydice. In Romano-British art of the early fourth century, he became the symbol of Christ, the Good Shepherd.
PALLADIUM	A statuette of Pallas Athene, rescued from Troy by Aeneas.
PEGASUS	A winged horse, tamed by Bellerophon with the help of a golden bridle given to him by the gods.
PELTA(E)	Originally the shield of the Amazons, a race of females living near the Black Sea; also referred to as an axe head. In stylised form, widely used in Greek and Roman art.

184

PERSEUS

Greek hero. Sent to cut off the head of Medusa, he was given a mirror by Athene thus obviating his looking directly at Medusa, which would have turned him to stone. He subsequently delivered Andromeda from a sea monster.

PERSPECTIVE BOXES

PHRYGIAN CAP

Worn by inhabitants of Phrygia, a country in Asia Minor.

POMEGRANATE

Punica granatum (L). The fruit of a North African and west Asiatic tree, resembling an orange. Used in art forms as a symbol of eternal life.

POSEIDON

See Neptune.

RAINBOW PATTERN

ROMULUS & REMUS

Descendants of Aeneas. Romulus and his twin

brother Remus were suckled by wolves. They grew up and founded the city of Rome, but in a quarrel Romulus killed his brother, thus becoming the first of the legendary Kings of Rome.

SALTIRE

St Andrew's cross.

SATURN (Roman)

Cronus/Chronos (Greek). Father of Jupiter. Represents Saturday, *dies Saturni.*

SATYR (Greek)

Faun (Roman). Male follower of Dionysus/ Bacchus, with goat's legs and horns, curly hair, snub nose and pointed ears. Later depicted as a naked youth playing the flute and dancing with Maenads.

SCALE PATTERN

Sometimes the scales are laid in straight lines like tiles and sometimes they radiate in concentric circles. The pattern may come from bird feathers or fish scales.

SCROLL

Foliate or floral scroll. Used as a border pattern in many different forms, one of the most common being the ivy leaf and lotus bud scroll.

SCROLL, GUILLOCHE
BORDERED CIRCLES

SCROLL, LOTUS   See Lotus wreath.

SELENE   See Luna.

SEMELE (Greek)   Loved by Zeus, whom she begged to appear
                    before her in his divine form in the last months
                    of her pregnancy. He visited her as the god of
                    Thunder and she was immediately consumed by
                    lightning. Zeus snatched the unborn child,
                    Dionysus, and sewed him into his own thigh
                    until the time for his birth arrived, when he was
                    taken and nursed by Semele's sister, Ino.

SILENUS (Greek)   Teacher and companion of Dionysus. Rep-
                    resented as an old man holding a cup of wine.

SMILAX   *Smilax aspera* (L). A species of trailing plant
                    with leaves somewhat resembling the ivy, but
                    with tendrils springing from the main stem.
                    Used in Greek and Roman art and apparently
                    replaced by ivy leaves in Britain.

187

SOL (Roman)　　　　　　　Helios (Greek). God of the sun. Young and handsome, with a crown of light rays. Represents Sunday, *dies Dominica*.

SPANDREL　　　　　　　　The space between a circle and the angles of an enclosing square.

SQUARES, INTERLACED

SWASTIKA PATTERN　　　Also known as fret and Greek key pattern.

SWASTIKA, FLORAL

SWASTIKA, GREEK KEY

SWASTIKA, LOZENGE

SWASTIKA, PELTA-
DUPLEX

TANIT

Punic (Carthaginian) goddess. Represented by
the 'symbol of Tanit', a wedge or bottle-shape
surmounted by a disc from which it is often
separated by a horizontal line, the ends turned
at right angles like arms. Later identified with
the Roman Goddess Juno.

THESEUS

The Greek hero who killed the Minotaur in the
Cretan labyrinth.

THYRSUS

A wand formed by the stem of a large plant
tipped with leaves or a fir cone and bound with
ribbons. Carried by Bacchus and Maenads.
Sometimes used to disguise a spear.

TRIANGLES, COG
WHEEL

189

TRIANGLES, DOG'S
TOOTH

TRIANGLES, STEPPED

Also known as crow's step triangles.

TRIPTOLEMUS (Greek)

Son of the King of Attica, he was taught agriculture and given seed and the appropriate tools by Demeter/Ceres.

TRITON (Greek)

Son of Poseidon/Neptune, has the upper parts of a man and the lower parts of a fish.

TYCHE

See Fortuna.

URN

Also known as a cantharus.

URN, LOTUS

URN, PELTA with
CONVOLUTES

VENUS (Roman)

Aphrodite (Greek). Goddess of love and beauty. Born of the sea foam, hence her frequent representation naked with a sea shell, Tritons and fishes. Mother of Cupid. Represents Friday, *dies Veneris.*

VICTORIA (Roman)

Nike (Greek). Goddess of Victory, represented with wings and a laurel wreath.

VILLA

Farm or country house.

VIRTUS (Roman)

Personification of bravery in war. Represented with helmet, spear and sword.

WAVE CREST PATTERN

WAVE PATTERN, SHADED

WHIRLING WHEEL PATTERN

WINDS

Four busts, often shown with up-standing hair and carrying a conch shell.

ZEUS (Greek)

See Jupiter.

'Z' PATTERN

ACKNOWLEDGEMENTS

A book of this kind can only be written with the help and co-operation of a great number of individuals and institutions.

I am especially indebted to George C. Boon, who has read the manuscript and contributed criticism, suggestions and, above all, encouragement, and also to Professor Jocelyn Toynbee, who has added her valuable advice on the contents of the Introduction and the Glossary. I should like to emphasise that any errors and omissions are mine.

My particular thanks go to Roger Peers and the Staff of the Dorset County Museum and to the Staff of the Dorset County Library, from all of whom I have received every possible assistance.

I am indebted to H.S.L. Dewar, who has given me constant support, and to all of the following: Mrs Madeleine Ackroyd-Simpson, Society of Antiquaries of London, Ashmolean Museum, Oxford, F.T. Baker, Cefni Barnett, John Bartlett, Mrs C.M. Bennett, Dr Keith Branigan, J.B. Calkin, Miss Dorothy Charlesworth, George Clarke and a boy of Stowe School, Colchester & Essex Museum, D.B. Connah, David Dawson, A.P. Detsicas, Alec Down, Miss B.R.K. Dunnett, Dr G.C. Dunning, R.A.H. Farrar, L.R. Fennelly, Anthony Fleming, W. Ford, Messrs. J.S. Fry & Sons (Somerdale), L.E.W.O. Fullbrook-Leggatt, P. Garrod, Gloucester City Library, R. Goodburn, C.N. Gowing, Captain H.S. Gracie, E. Greenfield, the Viscountess Hanworth, L.C. Hayward, Hereford City Library, L.W. Hoskins, Dr A.W.J. Houghton, F.R. Hughes, M.R. Hull, Michael Ingram, N. Irvine, F. Jenkins, D.E. Johnston, Leicester Museums, Lincoln City Museum, Miss Joan Liversidge, R.N. Lucas, C.L. Matthews, Alan McWhirr, R. Merrifield, Mrs Henrietta Miles, Miss Louise Millard, A.T. Morley Hewitt, D.S. Neal, W.E. Novis, Oxford City & County Museum, K.S. Painter, D.F. Petch, Mrs S.H.M. Pollard, W.G. Putnam, P. Rahtz, Reading Museum, Miss Mary Rennie, Richard Reece, J.F. Rhodes, Miss K.M. Richardson, Mrs Margaret Rule, I.F. Sanders, H. de S. Shortt, Dr D.J. Smith, Somerset County Museum, T.M. Staples, Dr I.M. Stead, J. Stevens Cox, D.S. Stewart, Sir Spencer Summers, D.J. Tomalin, Verulamium Museum, David Viner, J.S. Wacher, His Grace the 7th Duke of Wellington, David Whitehouse, J.B. Whitwell, Winchester City Museums, Wyndham Museum (Yeovil), Yorkshire County Library, Yorkshire Museum.

This book could not have been written without Alison Coate, who has not only given me every encouragement and worked hard to provide me with the leisure to accomplish the task in a very short space of time, but has also driven me all over the country to carry out research, taken photographs for my records and has typed the manuscript.

Boswells, Dorset 1972   A.R.

SELECTED BIBLIOGRAPHY

Bath
Cunliffe, Barry   *Roman Bath* (Society of Antiquaries Research
                          Report XXIV) Oxford 1969

Bignor
Winbolt, S.E. & Herbert G.   *The Roman Villa at Bignor, Sussex* 1934

Caerleon
Boon, G.C.   *Isca, The Fortress of the Second Augustan
                          Legion* Cardiff 1972

Caerwent

                          Archaeologia XXXVI (1856) LVII (1901) LVIII
                          (1902-3) LIX (1904-5) LX (1906-7) LXI (1909)
                          LXII (1910-11 LXIV (1913) LXXX (1930)

Colchester
Hull, M.R.   *Roman Colchester* (Society of Antiquaries
                          Research Report XX) Oxford 1958

Fishbourne
Cunliffe, Barry   'Excavations at Fishbourne' in *Antiquaries
                          Journal* XLII-XLV 1962-5
Cunliffe, Barry   *Excavations at Fishourne 1961-1969* (Society
                          of Antiquaries Research Report XXVI) Oxford
                          1971

Gloucester
Fullbrook-Leggatt,   *Roman Gloucester (Glevum)* Stroud 1968
L.E.W.O.

London
Merrifield, Ralph   *The Roman City of London* 1965

SELECTED BIBLIOGRAPHY
Lullingstone
Meates, G.W.   *Lullingstone, Roman Villa* 1955
Silchester
                                    Archaeologia LII-LXI 1890-1909
Boon, G.C.   *Roman Silchester* 1957 & revised edition
                                    forthcoming
Verulamium
Frere, S.S.   'Excavations at Verulamium' in *Antiquaries
                                    Journal* XXXVII-XXXIX 1957-9

General
Barley, M.W. & Hanson,
R.P.C. (ed)   *Christianity in Britain, 300-700* 1968
                                    Camden's Britannia 1695
Cottrell, L.   *Seeing Roman Britain* 1956
Frere, S.S.   *Britannia* 1967
Hinks, R.P.   *Catalogue of the Greek, Etruscan and Roman
                                    Paintings and Mosaics in the British Museum*
                                    1933
Kendrick, T.D.   *Anglo-Saxon Art to A.D. 900* 1938
Larousse   *Encyclopedia of Mythology* 1959
Lewis, M.J.T.   *Temples in Roman Britain* Cambridge 1966
Liversidge, Joan   *Britain in the Roman Empire* 1968
Lyell, A.H.   *A Bibliographical List. Description of Romano-
                                    British Architectural Remains in Great Britain*
                                    Cambridge 1912
Margary, I.D.   *Roman Roads in Britain* I-II 1955-7
Morgan, Thomas   *Romano-British Mosaic Pavements* 1886
Ordnance Survey   *Map of Roman Britain* 3rd edition 1956
Quennell, M. & C.H.B.   *Everyday Life in Roman Britain* 1952
Richmond, I.A.   'The Four Coloniae of Roman Britain' in
                                    Archaeologia CIII 1947
Richmond, I.A.   *Roman Britain* 2nd edition 1964
Rivet, A.L.F.   *Town and Country in Roman Britain* 2nd
                                    editon 1964
Rivet, A.L.F. (ed)   *The Roman Villa in Britain* 1969
RCHM (England)   *Inventory of the Historical Monuments in
                                    London* III (Roman) 1928
RCHM (England)   *Inventory of the Historical Monuments in the
                                    City of York* I *Eburacum, Roman York* 1962
Toynbee, J.M.C.   'Christianity in Roman Britain' in *Journal of
                                    the British Archaeological Association* (3rd
                                    series) XVI 1953

Toynbee, J.M.C.   *Art in Roman Britain* 2nd edition 1963
Toynbee, J.M.C.   *Art in Britain under the Romans* Oxford 1964
Wacher, J.S.   *The Civitas Capitals of Roman Britain*
                  Leicester 1966
Webster, Graham   *The Roman Army* 1956

ABBREVIATIONS USED FOR SOURCES

Ant J — *Antiquaries Journal*
Arch — *Archaeologia*
Arch Camb — *Archaeologia Cambrensis*
Arch Cant — *Archaeologia Cantiana*
Arch J — *Archaeological Journal*
Artis (1828) — Artis, E.T. *The Durobrivae of Antoninus* 1828

Barley & Hanson (1968) — Barley, M.W. & Hanson, R.P.C. (ed) *Christianity in Britain, 300-700* 1968
BBCS — *Bulletin of the Board of Celtic Studies*
Beecham (1886) — Beecham, K.J. *History of Cirencester, the Roman City of Corinium* 1886
Beesley (1848) — Beesley, A. *The History of Banbury* 1848
Berks AJ — *Berkshire Archaeological Journal*
BFC — *Bath Field Club Proceedings*
BMQ — *British Museum Quarterly*
Boon (1957) — Boon, G.C. *Roman Silchester* 1957 and revised edition forthcoming
Boon (1960) — Boon, G.C. *Isca* Cardiff 1960
Boon (1972) — Boon, G.C. *Isca, the Fortress of the Second Augustan Legion* Cardiff 1972
Branigan (1971) — Branigan, K. *Latimer* Bristol 1971
Britannia — *Britannia*. A Journal of Romano-British and Kindred Studies
Buckman & Newmarch (1850) — Buckman, J. & Newmarch, C.H. *Illustrations of the Remains of Roman Art in Cirencester* 1850
Builder — *The Builder, an Illustrated Weekly Magazine for the Architect, Engineer, Archaeologist, Constructor and Artist*

Charlesworth (1970) — Charlesworth, D. *Aldborough, Roman Town* 1970
Cunliffe (1969) — Cunliffe, Barry *Roman Bath* (Society of Antiquaries Research Report XXIV) Oxford 1969
Cunliffe (1971) — Cunliffe, Barry *Excavations at Fishbourne 1961-1969* (Society of Antiquaries Research Report XXVI) Oxford 1971

Down & Rule (1971) — Down, A. & Rule, N. *Chichester Excavations I*

(Chichester Civic Society) 1971

Fowler (1796-1818)

Fowler, W. *Engravings of the Principal Mosaic Pavements* Winterton 1796-1818

Fullbrook-Leggatt (1968)

Fullbrook-Leggatt, L.E.W.O. *Roman Gloucester (Glevum)* 1968

Gents Mag

Gentleman's Magazine

Gilyard-Beer (1951)

Gilyard-Beer, R. *The Romano-British Baths at Well* 1951

Hakewill (1826)

Hakewill, H. *An Account of the Roman Villa discovered at North Leigh, Oxon.* 1826

Hinks (1933)

Hinks, R.P. *Catalogue of the Greek, Etruscan & Roman Paintings in the British Museum* 1933

Hoare (1819)

Hoare, R. Colt *The History of Ancient Wiltshire II (Roman Aera)* 1819

Hull (1958)

Hull, M.R. *Roman Colchester* (Society of Antiquaries Research Report XX) Oxford 1958

Hutchins 3rd ed II (1863)

Hutchins, J. *History of Dorset* 3rd edition Vols 1-4 1861-70

Jack (1916)

Jack, G.H. *Woolhope Club Research Report* 1916

JBAA

Journal of the British Archaeological Association

JRS

Journal of Roman Studies

LAAS

Lincolnshire Architectural & Archaeological Society Reports & Papers

London in Roman Times

Wheeler, R.E.M. *London in Roman Times* (London Museum Catalogue No 3) 1930

Lysons (1797)

Lysons, S. *An account of Roman Antiquities discovered at Woodchester in the County of Gloucester* 1797

Lysons I (1813)

Lysons, S. *Reliquiae Britannico-Romanae* I 1813

Lysons II (1817)

Lysons, S. *Reliquiae Britannico-Romanae* II 1817

Lysons III (1817)

Lysons, S. *Reliquiae Britannico-Romanae* III (1817)

Meates (1955)

Meates, G.W. *Lullingstone Roman Villa* 1955

Merrifield (1965)	Merrifield, R. *The Roman City of London* 1965
Morgan (1886)	Morgan, Thomas *Romano-British Mosaic Pavements* 1886
Morley Hewitt (1969)	Morley Hewitt, A.T. *Roman Villa, West Park, Rockbourne* 1969
PDNHAFC	*Proceedings of the Dorset Natural History and Archaeological Field Club*
PDNHAS	*Proceedings of the Dorset Natural History & Archaeological Society*
PPHFC	*Papers and Proceedings of the Hampshire Field Club*
PSAL	*Proceedings of the Society of Antiquaries of London*
PSANHS	*Proceedings of the Somerset Archaeological & Natural History Society*
PSIA	*Proceedings of the Suffolk Institute of Archaeology*
RCHM	Royal Commission on Historical Monuments (England)
RCHM York I (1962)	RCHM (England) *Inventory of the Historical Monuments in the City of York:* I, *Eburacum, Roman York* 1962
Richmond (1963)	Richmond, I.A. *The Roman Pavements from Rudston* (Hull Museum Publications) 1963
Rudder (1833)	Rudder, S. *History of Cirencester* 1833
SDNQ	*Notes and Queries for Somerset & Dorset*
Smith, C.R. (1848)	Smith, C. Roach *Collectanea Antiqua* I 1848
Smith, D.J. (1965)	Smith, D.J. 'Three Fourth-Century Schools of Mosaic in Roman Britain' in Stern (ed) *La Mosaique Greco-Romaine* Paris 1965
Smith, D.J. (Ant J 1969)	Smith, D.J. 'Cirencester, 1967-8, Eighth Interim Report' in *Ant J* XLIX 1969
Smith, D.J. (1969)	Smith, D.J. 'The Mosaic Pavements' in *The Roman Villa in Britain* (ed) A.L.F. Rivet 1969
Smith, H.E. (1852)	Smith, H. Eckroyd *Reliquiae Isurianae* 1852
Soc of Ant of London Top Colls (Red or Brown Port)	Society of Antiquaries of London. *Topographical Collections* (Red or Brown Portfolio)
SxAC	*Sussex Archaeological Collections*
SyAC	*Surrey Archaeological Collections*

TBGAS	*Transactions of the Bristol and Gloucester Archaeological Society*
TDA	*Transactions of the Devonshire Association*
TEAS	*Transactions of the Essex Archaeological Society*
TERAS	*Transactions of the East Riding Antiquarian Society*
TLAHS	*Transactions of the Leicestershire Archaeological and Historical Society*
Toynbee (1963)	Toynbee, J.M.C. *Art in Roman Britain* 2nd edition 1963
Toynbee (PDNHAS 1963)	Toynbee, J.M.C. 'The Christian Roman Mosaic, Hinton St. Mary, Dorset' in PDNHAS 85 1963
Toynbee (1964)	Toynbee, J.M.C. *Art in Britain under the Romans* Oxford 1964
Toynbee (JRS 1964)	Toynbee, J.M.C. 'A New Roman Mosaic Pavement found in Dorset' in JRS LIV 1964
Toynbee (1968)	Toynbee, J.M.C. 'Pagan Motifs and Practices in Christian Art and Ritual in Roman Britain' in *Christianity in Britain, 300-700* (ed) M.W. Barley & R.P.C. Hanson Leicester 1968
Trans Thoroton Soc	*Transactions of the Thoroton Society of Nottinghamshire*
VCH	The Victoria History of the Counties of England
Vetusta Monumenta	Society of Antiquaries of London *Vetusta Monumenta* I-VI 1720-1823
WAM	*Wiltshire Archaeological Magazine*
Watkin (1886)	Watkin, W.T. *Roman Cheshire* Liverpool 1886
Wheeler (1932)	Wheeler, R.E.M. & T.V. *Report on the Excavations of the Prehistoric, Roman and Post-Roman Site in Lydney Park, Gloucestershire* (Society of Antiquaries Research Report IX) Oxford 1932
Wheeler (1936)	Wheeler, R.E.M. & T.V. *Verulamium, a Belgic and Two Roman Cities* (Society of Antiquaries Research Report XI) Oxford 1936
Whitwell (1970)	Whitwell, J.B. *Roman Lincolnshire* II Lincoln 1970
YAJ	*Yorkshire Archaeological Journal*
York Museum Handbook (1891)	*A Handbook to the Antiquities in the Grounds and Museum of the Yorkshire Philosophical*

Yorks Phil Soc Proc

Society York 1891
Proceedings of the Yorkshire Philosophical Society 1849-54

ABBREVIATIONS USED IN GAZETTEER

cent	century
f	found
exc	excavated
pl	plate
fig	figure
(?)	no positive evidence
os	old series
ns	new series

INDEX